A POCKETFUL OF M

ROWLEY

(MILESTONES OF MEMORY)

IRENE M DAVIES

THE KATES HILL PRESS

First Published By THE KATES HILL PRESS
39 Cowley Drive, Dudley, DY1 2SS

ISBN: 978 1 904552 45 1

British Library CIP Data:
A catalogue record for this book is available
from the British Library

Printed By: Lightning Source UK, Milton Keynes

Cover Design By: Greg Stokes
Cover Photograph: The Post Office at Springfield
From Sandwell Libraries Collection. All photographs reproduced with
kind permission of Sandwell Libraries.

A POCKETFUL OF MEMORIES – ROWLEY

Illustrations:-

Following the death of Dad in 1975, Irene M Davies was encouraged to write the experiences of her childhood and youth down by the children in her family who had been brought up in a tradition where storytelling and music hall song was the norm. In so doing she produced not only a family history, but also a history of her place, Rowley Village, and her time. Originally entitled Milestones of Memory, the work has been added to over the years. The Christmas chapter in particular has been expanded to incorporate the six Christmas stories by Irene that have appeared in The Black Country Bugle, one of which filled the front page. Milestones of Memory has been used in schools as a valuable aid to understanding the social history of the Black Country.

TO

LESLEY and MARTYN

DAVID, ANDREW and TIM

A POCKETFUL OF MEMORIES

This series brings to life the sights, sounds, and smells of a bygone age through the words of writers for whom those times were a reality.
The texts are complemented by period photographs or drawings of the area.

Also available:
A Pocketful of Memories - Blackheath
By Tossie Patrick (illustrated by Ron Slack)
A5 booklet, 32 pages, £2.50, ISBN 0 9520317 3 6

A Pocketful of Memories - Acock's Green
By Julia Waring
A5 booklet, 52 pages, £3.00, ISBN 1 904552 12 9

A Pocketful of Memories - Coseley
By Raymond Smout
A5 booklet, 52 pages, £3.00, ISBN 978 1 904552 17 8

A Pocketful of Memories - War Memories
Edited by Greg Stokes
A5 booklet, 48 pages, £3.00, ISBN 978 1 904552 18 5

A Pocketful of Memories - Roseville
By Raymond Smout
A5 booklet, 40 pages, £3.00, ISBN 978 1 904552 26 0

FAMILY BACKGROUND

THE HADLEY FAMILY

Rowley Village, Rowley Regis. Well the road still bears the same name, but a stranger could be forgiven for thinking that the name is something of a misnomer. There is nothing now to show that just a little while ago it really was a village. To stand in front of the Church and look towards Blackheath, one sees rows of neat modern houses stretching away into the distance, bordering the road like a pretty edge to a ribbon, and to right, and to left, more roads, and more houses, with no evidence left of the peaceful fields which once lay there. Once houses, cottages, villas, all nestling cheek by jowl with one another, in disorderly array, and reaching out from the Church down the hill to the public house known as the 'Sir Robert Peel', was officially Rowley Village proper, but the clusters of houses in Bell End, Siviter's Lane, Church Road, and Hawes Lane, would have comprised the Village in earlier times, with the road now known as Rowley Village, as the main road, or High Street.

Into this road, at number 86, was born on the last day of May 1895, a son, to Sarah, nee Taylor, and Arthur Hadley. He was named Samuel, and although he did not realize it, he had brothers and sisters older than himself. Tom, Alf, Horace, and George; and Emily, Sarah Ann, and Mary Ann, in the fashion of the times, Pem, Sairann, and Polly. By the time he was old enough to understand things, Tom was married to Ellen, (Nell), Alf was married to Ruth, and Emily was married to Jack Guest, who was also known as 'Joe the Lamplighter', he had also acquired a new baby brother, Wilfred, to say nothing of the fact that he had also become an uncle once or twice, but he was still too young to appreciate this news.

This little house stood approximately where Billington's chemist shop now stands, and it seems to have been unusual because it was the only double fronted house in the row. The fronts were brick faced, but at the back they were lumps of 'Rowley Rag', our local granite. The interior followed the usual pattern for those days, Ingle-nook fireplace, with a pantry door next to it with a 'glory-hole' above it penetrating underneath the stairs. The next door was the stair's door, and when you lifted the latch they revealed a steep flight of uneven, deep-treaded, corkscrew shaped stairs. These opened out into the main bedroom, and as it was a double-fronted house, two more bedrooms, one front and one rear, opened out from this.

Some of the houses, built at a later date, were all brick. They were higher, and always seemed to be built a few feet nearer to the road than the cottages, as though to show off their superiority. At the backs of the houses there was a brew house, cum scullery, (most families brewed their own beer, stout, or porter), with its large built-in copper for boiling the clothes. This demanded great attention on washdays. The fire underneath the boiler had to be lit at a very early hour to provide enough hot water for the maiding tub, and the rubbing tub, before being filled again for the actual boiling of the clothes. Next to the boiler, and sharing the same chimney was the baking oven, a very large affair this. Most people had big families to feed and usually baked one day per week so it was essential to make sure that enough loaves were made throughout the week.

A large iron mangle with heavy wooden rollers stood against the wall, near to the sink. The sink itself cannot be compared to anything known as a sink in a modern kitchen. These sinks were made of bricks, being more like a table top than anything else. Useful for standing a bowl on, or the rubbing tub. An arched alcove in the centre below the sink left room for a galvanized bucket to stand. Nails, or hooks knocked into the wall held a small bath, and a colander, or other small tools. A shelf across the wall carried the various sizes of heavy cast iron cooking utensils. Some had the familiar long handles, these stood on the hob; and some had handles over the top, and these could be slung over the fire on gale hooks, or pot hooks, attached to the crane, or gate fixed on the side of the fire grate. A small hand bowl with a wooden handle used for hand washing, or ladling water from the boiler, was usually left upside down in the sink when not in use.

There was no running water in the brew house. There was only one tap in the yard. A large affair on a stand pipe, in their case shared by some half dozen houses, but on some yards by many more. Even this was a 'modern' innovation. Formerly all drinking water had had to be fetched from the nearest spring. Granny Hadley told me that this was down Moor Lane, a very long journey indeed, especially on cold winter mornings. Beyond the brew house was the inevitable nail shop. Privies were not so private. Shared yards shared these too. There were no dustbins, they had ash pits.

Inside the cottages the furniture was sparse. Children were usually many. The bedrooms were quite small, and low. Generally there would be two beds to each room, often three or four children sleeping in each bed. A tin trunk or wooden chest to hold spare clothes, if they were lucky, or spare bedclothes, if they were luckier still. A curtain on a piece of string across a recess hid any out-door clothes not in use. A few nails knocked in the wall served as hangers. Sometimes in the main bedroom a small wooden chest with a cheval mirror balanced on top served as a dressing table. The only form of lighting was a candle, or a paraffin lamp.

The living room had a large white wood table which required much scrubbing to keep it clean. Dad said that the table had to be well scrubbed because dinners would be served directly on to the wood in lots of cases, with a hole left in the centre for gravy, or else a thick slice of bread, sometimes dipped into the meat tin. Meat was often only served to the men folk. A piece of 'dip' was served to the children. A few wooden chairs, some known as lath-backed, wheel-backed, Windsor chairs, and ladder backed, all were popular at that time. On one wall would be a large chest of drawers. A lace-edged cover on top. At the back, the children's Sunday School prizes were stacked up in neat rows. In the middle a Victorian glass centre-piece flanked by a pair of large Staffordshire pottery dogs, or large glass bells. Stuffed birds or animals in glass domes were also very popular. Pushed into the inglenooks on either side of the fireplace were wooden 'screens'. These were seats with very high backs, useful for screening out draughts and making the fireplace seating area snug and warm. The seat was usually covered with a long soft pad to make it more comfortable to sit upon, and a deep frill extending to the floor concealed the storage drawers underneath the seat. The floor was red quarry tiles. Floor coverings were podged rugs. These were made during long winter evenings. All the family could join in. Any clothes that were out-grown, or out worn, were stored in a large rag-bag, then, when enough had been collected they were cut into small pieces, and with a podging tool, pushed into Hessian, a large sugar bag from the grocers being the handiest thing. Sometimes a simple pattern was marked out on the Hessian, other times random podging gave a marbled effect. In any case a good warm rug was made. When finished they were brushed over with a paste made from flour and water, or with thick starch, or size; this stiffened the back and helped stop the pieces from working loose. Then a backing of plain Hessian was stitched into place. They were very heavy when they were new.

At the back of the houses, beyond the brew houses, was the yard. Not much in the way of gardens. The men who were interested in gardening usually rented an allotment so that they could grow their own vegetables. Most kept a few hens in a coop, and a pig or two, or went shares with a friend who had more room. Most women seemed to do a stint each day in the nail shop, and Granny Hadley was no exception. Life was most difficult for a woman in those days.

She was a remarkable woman. As a child, her rather brusque manner frightened the life out of me, but as I grew older, and especially after she broke her leg when she was about eighty years old, I came to know her better. She told me of the long hours which she had to work. Washing and cooking for the family. Doing her stint in the nail shop, often times to within a few hours of another confinement; of getting up again too soon, and getting back to the nail shop. Attending to the new baby as best she could, and the next eldest having to mind the baby in between whiles. She did not complain. It was the common lot. They needed the money badly, and if they did not turn out their quota for the week there may not be the metal allowed them for the next week, - and then where would they be? The children learned to pick up the nails as soon as they were big enough.

Saturday nights the children were tubbed, literally, and dosed with brimstone and treacle, whether they needed it or not. Then they were put to bed while Granny washed their underclothes. In the belief that Cleanliness is next to Godliness, she made sure that no child of hers was going to Sunday School with soiled clothes. After all that she had to hurry down to Blackheath to try to get a joint of meat when the butchers were selling off cheaply near to closing time, around 10 O'clock. She went to chapel herself if possible on Sunday afternoon to the P.S.A., and to the service on Sunday nights.

Her energy, or her will power, was enormous. When there was anything they particularly needed from Birmingham she would get up at four to do the washing and cleaning. Walk to Birmingham, going down Mincing Lane, cross over what is now the Birmingham/Wolverhampton New Road, passed Lightwoods Park to Bearwood, and on to Birmingham Bull Ring. She lost me at Bearwood because the way she described was all fields and open paths, and it was all built up in my time. After buying her goods she walked back in time to do her stint in the nail shop. In addition to all this day to day running of her own household, she was very popular in cases of illness. Confinements, sickness, sitting-up with the very ill, and laying-out if they died. I found it rather touching when she spoke about this. There were no chapels of ease, or whatever the undertakers care to call them. a body was laid out at home, and stayed there until the day of the funeral. There would be visits from friends and neighbours to inspect the body, not out of inquisitiveness, but to pay their last respects and to show sympathy for the bereaved family. It was usually because of this that no matter how patched or worn their nightdresses were a good one was usually laid aside, clean and ironed so that they looked respectable laid out. It was the same with sheets, and if there were no good ones, or any considered good enough, some friendly neighbour who had, quietly loaned theirs until after the funeral.

Her faith in God was both simple and strong. To her He was very real, and very near. She talked to Him, and of Him, as though He was a real live friend; taking to Him all her troubles, and all her fears, quite certain that He would listen, and equally certain that He would find the right solution. She was satisfied that He always would. I was always reminded of the phrase, 'Unless ye come to me as a little child'.

Grandad Hadley I never knew as he died before I was born. He was a bricklayer by trade, and seemingly a good one. Perhaps not very fond of beer, but more taken with wines and spirits I believe. This was probably where a lot of his wages went, but Granny never complained to me, she did not believe in speaking ill of the dead; and Dad, who was practically teetotal, only said that he had seen too much of the evils of drink to want to start himself.

I think he came from Oldbury. Certainly he could read and write, which was very rare in his youth. If anyone received a letter it was often Grandad who read it for them, and sent a reply. He kept racing pigeons, and liked to win. If he could catch a rival's bird which had arrived home before his, he was not averse to trapping it until after his own had arrived home. For this he earned the nick-name of Arthur Trapper. He died from cancer in 1916.

Childhood was not easy by the sound of it. Dad said that everyone had their chores to attend to, even helping in the nail shop, and there was no shirking. Granny would stand no nonsense, and who could blame her? After hitting Uncle George over the head with a cast iron saucepan for some misdemeanour she examined it closely and then declared, 'If yo'd a med it run out m'lad, I shouldn't half a-paled thee' Such rough justice was taken with good grace, with no hard feelings on either side.

Of course, things that were happening in the outside world reached here too. Dad remembered how little things stood out in his mind. Odd words, like Lord Kitchener, the Battle of Omdurman, the Dervishes, the Boer War, the Relief of Ladysmith, and of Mafeking. He had started to go to school. In the old Parochial Hall and the children had to pay two pence per week. It seems to have been a penny reading and a penny for writing. At about this time too, around 1900, Dad said that the sewers were laid in Rowley and they dug up the floor of the house to lay them.

Later Dad attended the school at Hawes Lane. This was a Church of England School and came under the jurisdiction of the Vicar. This was one long room divided off for classes with curtains. Mr. Swallow was the headmaster. I believe he came originally from Netherton, but when I knew him he lived in Siviter's Lane. After he retired he went to live Malvern way. A younger brother of his worked at the same time as Dad at British Cyanides, later British Industrial Plastics Ltd., Oldbury. He was one of the managers I think. Another of the teachers was Miss. Maud Edwards who lived next door to the school. She was still there when I went to Hawes Lane School. Later she married a Mr. Taylor.

Teaching was very strict. It probably had to be. Mr. Swallow was small in stature, but I understand he was quite capable of giving six of the best when necessary, and it was quite possible that if a child went home and complained he ran the risk of getting another hiding for not behaving himself. In the main however, an education was not greatly desired, and so most pupils went unwillingly to school, wanting only to learn enough to pass the required Standard to leave school and start work. Some managed this by the time they were ten others stayed until they were eleven or twelve. Later this was changed and they all had to stay until they were thirteen. Even so, it was not until 1911 that a Coal Mining Act was passed forbidding the employment of boys less than fourteen to work below ground, and less than twelve to work on the surface. There was plenty of industrial work in this area, and most had a job to go to as soon as they were able to get away from school.

Perhaps because Grandad Hadley could read and write himself, and there were books in the house, the children were allowed to read and write themselves within certain limits. On the whole reading was regarded as a complete waste of time. This attitude persisted until the start of the Second World War, probably still does in some families. Whether this was due to the long hours of work which had been necessary to earn enough to keep body and soul together, I do not know, but, if anyone was seen with a book in their hands they were soon told to put it away and find something better to do. They were considered idle. To try to do more than was absolutely necessary to pass the required Standard to leave school altogether, was madness. Their outlook was so narrow in fact, that it was considered wrong to learn anything which would place you above your 'station'. Education was only for gentlefolk, and you must never think that you could be their equal in any way.

Fortunately, after the First World War, when more men folk had been abroad, there came a gradual awakening, and some people began to change their ideas. Some of the brighter children started to enter for examination, and after passing same, went on to Wright's Lane Secondary School, or to the Grammar Schools at Halesowen or Dudley, and books received as Sunday School prizes were read, instead of being stacked under lace covers on the chest of drawers.

I have said that Uncle Tom was married to Aunt Nell, well they lived in Whiteheath. It would be no use asking me the names of their children because as far as I can remember I only knew two, Joe and Mary. There were some seventeen of them and it always amazed me when I went to their house. They had a teapot that must have held thirty cups of tea, and a kettle to match. It took two children at a time to fill it.

The same goes for Uncle Alf and Aunt Ruth. I don't think I ever knew all the children. There were two about my age, Eva, and I think one was May. Aunt Emily and Uncle Jack had quite a family, Annie, Arthur, Sarah, John, Lily, George, Violet, Florence, and Joe. Uncle Horace and Aunt Mary Jane lived almost opposite Siviter's Lane. There was Lily, Sarah, Arthur, May, Doris and Stanley.

Aunt Sarah Ann was the most travelled of the family. She had been for a time a ladies maid. When she married Uncle Mark Rushton they went to live at Stourport. They had two children, Evelyn and Mark. For obvious reasons we did not see a great deal of them. Uncle Mark died when he was still young, Evelyn too after a short married life. Mark and his wife Margaret now live in America. Their son Christopher married an American girl. Uncle George worked for Stewarts and Lloyds and went to live in Corby with Aunt Hannah and the two boys when the new town was built. I never knew them well at all. Aunt Polly and Uncle Jack Southall went to live at 52 Hawes Lane, with Arthur and Jack Jr. Howard was born June 1929. This was my second home. If Mom was not in when I reached home I always fled to Aunt Polly. Uncle Wilf and Aunt Lil (Hilary) moved from Rowley Village into a council house at Whiteheath. They had four children, Hilary, Robert, David, and Jack. Robert was the only one I knew.

THE HODGETTS FAMILY

Lower down the hill lived the Hodgetts family. William, and his wife Sarah Ann, nee Molynieux, from Kate's Hill, Dudley. They had two sons, John and Richard, always known as Jack and Dick; and daughters, Eliza, Rebecca, Phoebe, Martha, and the youngest Sarah Ann. Granny Hodgetts never made nails to my knowledge, but she may have helped out with washing and baking for a family nearby. Grandad was a labourer at Doulton's. They were very gentle people. As a child I went there often for my dinner on Sundays. Sometimes I stayed there on Saturday nights, then I slept with Aunt Martha in her big bed.

They had a parlour and a living room, and at the rear a huge kitchen. Granny did not need to use this room for cooking because there was a half-range grate in the living room. Aunt Eliza and her family lived in this big kitchen. It must have been most inconvenient. The sleeping quarters must have been cramped too.

There was a lovely big garden to the rear of their house, with a cherry tree, pear and apple trees, and a mauve lilac bush. We didn't have a garden so I thought it was wonderful. I remember how I used to follow Grandad about when he was working in that garden. He was very patient with me, because I asked countless questions. Looking back now, I suppose it was Uncle Joe who did most of the work because Grandad must have been quite old then.

There must have been a flower bed or two, but I cannot remember them. There were a few gilly flowers, Granny's favourite, growing in the nooks and crannies of the old wall, but I remember the vegetables best. I remember the potatoes and peas, the celery in trenches, and the scarlet runner beans. The bean seed was never bought in a packet, but was carefully saved from the previous year. Bright pink and blue patterned, they looked beautiful when they were tipped out of the cocoa tin where they had slept all winter long. He used to talk to me as we planted the seed. Even now I remember that around here we should not plant beans before the twenty-third of May: and after dibbling the hole for potatoes, to sprinkle in a little sand to make a warm bed for the seed potatoes, so that they did not catch cold from the bottom; and I never see the big purple seed heads on the leeks without seeing him tying a paper bag over the top to save the seeds as they ripened.

In the early 1920's Uncle Jack Hodgetts and Aunt Lil moved to Highley. Much later on they moved to Kidderminster. They lived then in a bungalow on an estate almost opposite the British Sugar Corporation. I think they had two children but I only remember Lily.

Uncle Dick and Aunt Nance lived in Siviter's Lane where Aunt Nance kept a small drapers shop. They had three children. Alice, William and Ivy. Alice lives near to us in Fairway Avenue, and we see Horace, her husband, frequently, but I never see any of the others.

Aunt Eliza married Uncle Joe Davies, same surname as us, but no relation. She had five children. Lily, Bill, Bert, Dora and Gwen. As I have already told you they were living at Granny's house. Dora is exactly seven weeks younger than me so I had more to do with her than with the others.

Aunt Beck had married a miner from Yorkshire, Uncle Bill Wroe. At one time they went to live in Yorkshire but returned later to live some three doors up the hill from Granny Hadley's, and next door incidentally to Jethro Sidaway, the only Rowley man alive in my day who had lived to see all four of the Rowley Churches. They had five children also. Dennis, the same age as Aunt Eliza's Lily, Leonard, Tom, Arthur, and Doris. She was five years older than I was and Arthur was one year older.

Aunt Phoebe married Jack Mullett from Blackheath; he also was a miner. with his two brothers he emigrated to America. After they had found work and established themselves they sent for their wives and families. Aunt Phoebe had a little girl already, also named Lily, and they sailed from Liverpool, for America in 1912. She had two more children, Irene and Clarence. Unfortunately, Uncle Jack was killed in a mining accident a few years later, and eventually she married Francis Westwood. He too was a miner, an American of British descent. She had four more daughters, Evelyn, Nellie, Millicent, and Lucille. Aunt Martha never married.

Then there was Mom; Sarah Ann, the youngest. She was born with one leg two inches shorter than the other. Nowadays I suppose something could be done by a good orthopaedic surgeon, but in 1894 this was not possible. For some years constant journeys were made to the Dispensary. There was no National Health Service in those days so she used to get taken in a push-chair to get free medical attention and an issue of cod liver oil. She never grumbled. She observed that in those days she was able to join in most of the games that the children played. She could run, jump, and skip, awkwardly maybe, but she managed well enough. She swayed badly as she walked, which was to affect her back in later years, but she never lacked courage, and always did her best to keep up with her playmates.

Mom did not go the Church of England School. The children from the lower end of the Village went to the .Endowed School. This stood in Birmingham Road opposite to Macmillan Road. This school was closed as a day school anyway when the new schools at Currall Road and Siviter's Lane were opened. Mom said the children were each given a stick of rock, and then marched in a crocodile up to the new schools.

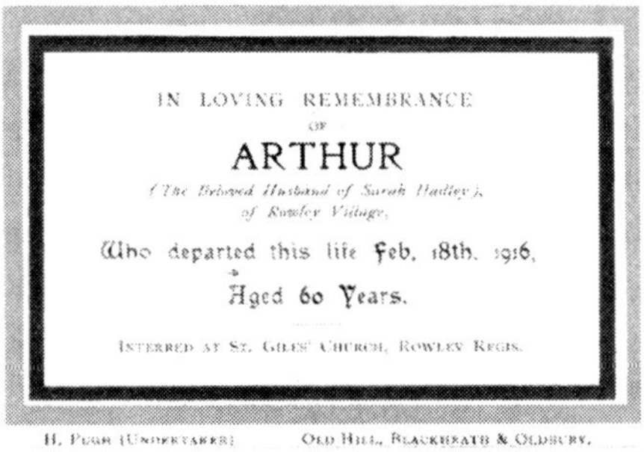

IN LOVING REMEMBRANCE

OF

ARTHUR

(The Beloved Husband of Sarah Hadley),
of Rowley Village,

Who departed this life Feb. 18th. 1916,

Aged 60 Years.

INTERRED AT ST. GILES' CHURCH, ROWLEY REGIS.

H. PUGH (UNDERTAKER) OLD HILL, BLACKHEATH & OLDBURY.

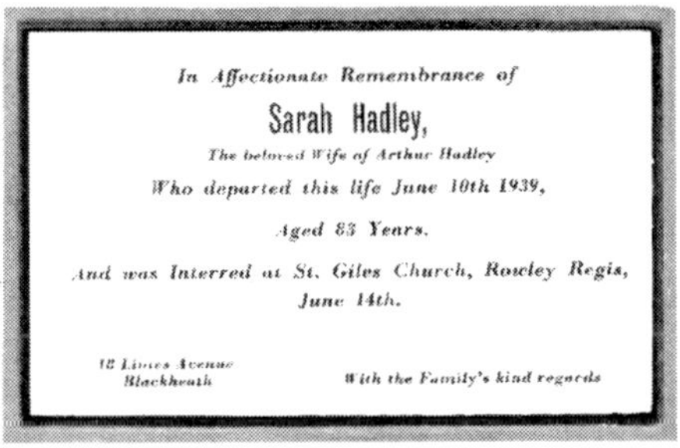

In Affectionate Remembrance of

Sarah Hadley,

The beloved Wife of Arthur Hadley

Who departed this life June 10th 1939,

Aged 83 Years.

And was Interred at St. Giles Church, Rowley Regis,
June 14th.

12 Limes Avenue
Blackheath

With the Family's kind regards

Family Death Notices
A tradition no longer practiced

Grandad Hadley
The only photograph of him ever taken
(death notice above)

COMMON BACKGROUND

Where Mom and Dad first met they never said, but they were from families who were 'Chapel'. Most families were either 'Church' or 'Chapel', so it is safe to assume that they knew each other from early Childhood.

Another common meeting ground was on the road to Doulton's. Like most children, one of the daily chores was taking dinners. No works canteens in those days. Hot dinners were carried to the works in basins, a saucer fitted over the top, sometimes holding a thick slice of bread, and tied up tightly with a red and white spotted handkerchief. There was a terrible row if one failed to be at the gate when the hooter, or 'bull' went. It was a task carried out by each successive child down to the youngest. When there were no more children, a neighbour's child was paid a few coppers each week to take on the job. It was hard work, especially in the winter. Some children took more than one dinner and they often only had time to have a 'piece' for their own dinner. This was usually a thick slice of bread, spread with potato, or swede and potato mashed together, or sometimes sausage.

Mom took Grandad's, Dad took Strat Parkes', Jimmy Perry's, Frank Low's, Mr. Darby's. and Uncle Alf's. These were at Sampson, Richards', the Hailstone, and Lake Quarries; and he took Billy Taylor's to Doulton's. I can only hope that they had different knocking-off times. However, to aid his progress he rode a black pony belonging to Parkes's bare back, and carrying all those dinners. I think he ought to have been in a circus.

He took Billy Taylor's to Doulton's last; and Mom used to say that they could hear the pony coming at full gallop down Doulton Road, with Dad hugging the basin tightly to his chest so as not to spill the gravy, and everyone calling, 'Hi up! Here comes Sammy on his hoss'!

The pony and Dad had an affinity with each other. If anyone left the door open he would come in and try to get up the stairs to get to Dad. Granny Hadley used to shriek, and Dad used to have to get over the pony's head to get it to back away and out of the house. Only Thelwell could do justice to such a situation!

By 1908 much had been happening. Queen Victoria's Jubilee had gone, - and so had Queen Victoria. Granny Hadley had a huge portrait of her over the fireplace at number 44, a house on the opposite side of the road to number 86. She had great respect for her. Now, her son, the former Prince of Wales, had become King Edward the Seventh. Granny was not amused. Seemingly she pursed her lips with disapproval when she heard his name. The old picture of his royal mother still reigned over the fireplace.

Shackleton had almost reached the South Pole. Marconi had transmitted Morse wireless signals from Cornwall to Newfoundland, and Mom and Dad had both left school.

Mom went to work at Perry's Pens. Later she was to leave and go to work for Armfields making buttons on a small hand press. Aunt Martha went to work there too and when Armfields closed down she moved from

Birmingham to Aston, to work for Buttons Limited. She stayed there until her retirement at sixty. Mom stayed at Armfields until a short time after she got married. It was not fashionable for married women to go out to work.

Dad went to work at T.P. Moyle's shop for a few weeks. It was on the corner of Church Road, almost opposite Rowley Church gates. I believe he had been an errand boy there previously, part time. He spent his time weighing-up the dry goods. Sugar, rice, dried peas, and such, and grinding coffee. The hours were long because most shops kept open very late. His wages were four shillings and sixpence per week. (22.5p in current coinage)

Eventually, Grandad told him that he was taking him to learn bricklaying. He found Grandad a very hard taskmaster. He never hesitated to kick over a wall that did not meet with his approval, but, he knew his job well and over the next seven years or so he gradually instructed Uncle Horace, Dad, and later Uncle Wilf, through all the grades of the building trade. Strangely enough, Dad and Uncle Horace, in 1915, connected the sewer at the old house to the mains. He said the manhole cover was right outside the back door.

They worked on brick graves, and tombs. They built the new wall around Rowley Church when the road was widened. Public houses, churches, chapels, private houses, chimney stacks, and down the mines. The latter was specialist work. The courses in the tunnels had to be laid in a slanting strengthening bond. They worked down several local pits. They had a lifelong habit of walking to work, and I have heard Dad say that after walking as far maybe as West Bromwich, they had to walk as far again underground, when they got out of the cage. Whilst they were working down one pit, I think it was Jubilee, but I am not certain, the pit flooded. Dad and Uncle Horace had to run to get the last cage up. Grandad did not follow them and later he came up the shaft hand over hand. His hands, and the inside of his legs were blistered and burned by the friction. He had been to let the pit ponies loose so that they could find their own way to higher ground.

During this seven year apprenticeship more changes were taking place. King Edward had gone to his ancestors on the sixth of May in 1910, and King George the Fifth and his wife, Princess May of Teck, to be known as Queen Mary, were now seated on the throne. A 2nd Son of King Edward, they were the former Duke and Duchess of York. Granny no longer pursed her lips and frowned, but she still kept Queen Victoria in state over the mantelpiece. The new monarchs would have to prove their worth. In that same year Halley's Comet had appeared in the sky, and a German Zeppelin had crashed. Dr. Crippen, the murderer, had been arrested on board ship, along with his female accomplice. The first criminals to be apprehended by use of the new-fangled wireless. The Duke of Cornwall was created Prince of Wales and Earl of Chester, and Winston Churchill was horse-whipped by a Suffragette.

Some years are memorable because of the many outstanding events which take place. 1911 was one of those years. Preparations were underway for the coronation of King George and Queen Mary; The Prince of Wales was created a Knight of the Garter, and in July the King and Queen made a Royal visit to Wales for the Investiture of the Prince of Wales at Caernarvon. The red Dragon of Wales was revived in his new Coat of Arms. On the Eleventh of November the King and Queen left England to travel to India to attend the Coronation Durbar at Delhi. It was a most sumptuous affair, and the announcement was made that henceforth Delhi was to be the capital of India in place of Calcutta.

The next year brought the tragic story of the so-called unsinkable 'Titanic'. There was much trouble in Ireland. There were many voices raised both for and against Home Rule; and the suffragettes were busy chaining themselves to railings and going on hunger strikes. One thing Dad would have been pleased about though - West Bromwich Albion won the Cup.* Over on the continent there was trouble in the Balkans. Turkey declared War on Bulgaria and Serbia.

It was February 1913 when the news arrived here of the death of Captain Scott and his companions on their return journey from the South Pole. We can imagine their disappointment when they reached the Pole to find that Captain Amundsden had reached there first. A suffragette threw herself in front of the King's horse at the Derby and was fatally injured. A few days later, eighteenth June, Rowley Church was badly damaged by fire. In July Romania declared War on Bulgaria, but by August they had all signed a Peace Treaty. In October the Panama Canal was officially opened.

Trouble in Ireland, and with the suffragettes continued in 1914. Mrs. Pankhurst was arrested for the eighth time in three years and sentenced. Eventually they ceased demonstrating. The end of June brought the news of the assassination of Archduke Franz Ferdinand of Austria and his wife at Sarajevo. A month later Austria declared War on Serbia. Germany supported Austria and Russia backed Serbia. France was an ally of Russia and joined in immediately.

It was Bank Holiday weekend in Britain. Mrs. Chater told me how they walked to Blackheath Station on Monday morning and went to Birmingham to visit Cannon Hill Park. They caught the tram back to town to catch a train from Snow Hill station, and walked into chaos. Reserves for the Navy and the Army had been recalled during the day, and the troop trains were pulling away from the station as quickly as possible. Civilians had to wait. Everyone knew now that War was inevitable. Germany marched into Belgium, and Britain could sit on the fence no longer, they jumped in on the side of the underdog. 11.30 p.m. Fourth of August 1914. Great Britain declared War against Germany.

The War, which everyone had confidentially expected to be over by Christmas, went rampaging on. Each new battle brought news of the terrible casualties. As the call went out for more and more gun-fodder the women gradually took over the men's jobs. 1915 dragged on, with Zeppelin raids on

**Sadly, they didn't. Barnsley beat them 1-0 in the final. Ed.*

various parts of the coast from Tyneside to Kent. Germany was blockading Britain and things were looking black.

Nurse Edith Cavell was shot on the seventh of October, and here at home Grandad Hadley was ill. The doctor diagnosed cancer, and suggested that the family call in a physician. This was done at no small expense. I think the fee was five guineas, (£5.25). but the weekly wage of the men was only about £1.00 to £1.50 so it was quite a lot of money to find. It was of no avail however, he confirmed the doctor's diagnosis and Grandad died on the eighteenth February 1916. He was sixty years of age.

A few Zeppelins had managed to reach the Midlands at the end of January, but it seems to have been an isolated case. Aunt Polly married Uncle Jack Southall, and conscription was brought into service. Now all single men between the 19-30 age group could be 'called up'. The death rate was alarming. The Battle of the Somme alone, which lasted from July to November, killed some half million British men. The names of places abroad took on a familiar ring as the state of the war was discussed. Turkey, Gallipoli, Constantinople, and the Dardanelles, in the East, and the Somme, Ypres, Boulogne and the like nearer home.

There had been a lot more trouble in Ireland. The Easter week brought the trouble with the Sinn Fein to a head, and rebellion raged. Sir Roger Casement was arrested, sentenced to death, and hanged on the third of August. He was charged with treason. He had tried to enlist German aid in the Sinn Fein cause.

More women were joining the Army, (WAACS), Navy, (WRENS), and the Land Army. This was the year when tanks were first used too. They took the Germans by surprise. At the end of the year the monk Rasputin was murdered in Russia.

The food problem became worse and worse. The shops were practically empty and any food available was very expensive. Partial rationing came into force in June 1917, and general rationing six months later. The shortage was caused by the intense blockade. There had been fierce sea battles waged, but Germany was carrying out a policy of 'unrestricted submarine warfare', and many merchant ships were sunk.

America declared War on Germany in April, but it was the end of June before her troops landed in France. Parts of the coast were shelled from the sea, and London was being bombed. In the Middle East, Jerusalem surrendered to the British. The Holy City was ours. Russia was temporarily out of the War. They were having a Revolution.

Mom and Dad were married in July. Weddings in those days were quiet affairs. No white dresses and veils. Just a new dress and a new hat, and the couple walked to church. Sometimes a few friends accompanied them, then they walked back home again. The wedding breakfast, if any, was very modest, and normal life was resumed immediately. Dad, and lots of other people at this stage of the War, had to go to work, wedding or no wedding; but he was given a nice clock as a wedding present by his workmates at

British Cyanides.

They shared the house in the village with Aunt Polly, Uncle Jack, and their baby, Arthur. After the War this house was to become the butcher's shop owned by Albert Taylor, cousin to Aunt Polly and Dad, his father being a brother of Granny Hadley. The shop window faced right across Currall Road, but this was an alteration. The original house looked out over the village, down the hill to Blackheath. It was a large rambling house which must I think have been the lodge or coach house to the big house next door. I say 'big' because when it was new it must have been one house. Indeed, I understand that at one time it was a coaching inn. At sometime a second front door had been added, different to the original, and it made two houses. Mr. Frank Taylor, Albert's brother, lived in part and he said that it was on his deeds that it was a coaching inn, but of course I never saw the deeds myself.

Mom must have been glad that she was not alone in that house. The War was really hotting up. Germany tried very hard to gain ground before the fresh troops from America could become effective. They used Liquid Fire at Cambrai, and Mustard Gas was also used, and Allied casualties were very heavy. I don't know what Dad was doing either. He was gassed seventeen times, and he lost his sense of smell.

Uncle Jack Guest, and Uncle Jack Hodgetts were in the Forces, and finally Uncle Wilf was called up. Dad had not passed his medical because of his eyes, that was why he was working at British Cyanides. Uncle Jack Southall worked there too.

When 1918 dawned the Air Forces of both sides were becoming more daring. Air raids, and counter attacks, as each tried to defend their own troops, and air raids over enemy territory. Shells from a huge gun nick-named 'Big-Bertha' fell on Paris, fired by the Germans from Coucy, some seventy miles away.

At the Battle of the Marne however, German advance was stemmed. The tide had turned, slowly but surely the war machine was grinding to halt. Finally, it was all over. At the eleventh of the eleventh day of the eleventh month, all hostilities ceased. The War was over. News did not travel so speedily then as now. Rumours had been flying about thick and fast, that a truce had been declared, but no one seemed to know for certain. I remember Miss Harrison telling us in class that she was just leaving Birmingham Art Gallery when the news was broken to the crowd waiting around the Council House in Victoria Square. She said that within a few seconds everything was bedlam. People were singing and dancing in the street. Tramcar's bells were clanging, people were leaning out of office windows cheering and waving to the crowds below. Shaking hands with complete strangers, hugging and kissing, laughing and crying, so relieved were they by the news. Lots of people left their jobs to rush home to tell their families that the War was at an end. The price of war is always high.

The Rev. G.A. Studdart-Kennedy, better known as 'Woodbine Willie', from his habit of giving a Woodbine cigarette to the troops, wrote a poem that is very appropriate:

WASTE

Waste of Muscle, waste of Brain,
Waste of Patience, waste of Pain,
Waste of Manhood. waste of Health,
Waste of Blood, and waste of Tears,
Waste of Youth's most precious years,
Waste of ways the saints have trod,
Waste of Glory, waste of God---
War!

Not so much talked about maybe was the world wide influenza epidemic. An estimated 20 million people died.

Back Row: Sarah, Uncle Horace, Lily, Arthur
Front Row: May, Stanley, Aunt Mary, Doris

AFTER THE WAR

I was born shortly before the end of the War. I cannot say that I was born and bred in Rowley because I wasn't. Bred, yes, but I did not arrive here until I was six weeks old. The word today is 'adoption', but was usually 'took to' then. It was fairly common. If a woman died, and children were left orphaned, relatives or friends befriended the children. 'Took- to' is a much warmer expression I think than is adoption. Mom and Dad named me Irene after Irene Mullett in America. In this year of peace they did not realize that Irene is the Greek word for 'Peace'.

When the house opposite became vacant, next door to Ben Tibbetts' shop, Mom applied for it to the owner, Mr. Tom Williams who was well known in these parts. The application was successful and we moved in. Our house and the one next door had once been business premises. Ours was the house and next door had been the shop, but now they were two separate houses sharing the same yard. We had two large living rooms and a washhouse, with a boiler and a baking oven, a sink with a tap, and an indoor flushing toilet. This was luxury.

Upstairs there was one front bedroom, one rear bedroom over the rear living room, and three steps down from this was another bedroom over the back kitchen of the house next door. We never used this as a bedroom, but in the summer I used to go up there to sit in the deep window embrasure. It used to catch the last rays of the dying sun up there and I could see to read for ages after darkness had drawn in downstairs. When Mr. and Mrs. Truman lived with us Mr. Truman used this window embrasure as a table. He used to like repairing clocks and watches, and this extra light was ideal.

I never remember us having oil lamps for lighting although both Grannies did. There was gaslight in this house. We had a pilot light in the main living room and you only had to pull the 'On' chain and the gas lit. If you had to light gas with a match or taper it was very easy to poke the mantle and break it. The ceiling above the light used to get very dirty from the gas light which wasn't in the middle of the ceiling but hung over the middle of the dining table. When Mr. Cole, the painter and decorator from Siviter's Lane, came to decorate the room I was surprised to see the size of his scissors. They were the largest I had ever seen. After he had whitened the ceiling he placed a large circular shiny paper around the ceiling rose. This could be wiped over with a soapy cloth and helped protect the ceiling from the smoky black stain.

Our next door neighbours were Mr. and Mrs Joe Chater and their young son, Leslie. They became 'Aunt' and 'Uncle' to all of us and remained so for the rest of their lives. Poor Leslie died when he was only six years old. I recall being taken to see him in his coffin and being made to touch his face. It was a common practice then. Another son, Harold, born later, died when only fourteen months old. They never had any more children. In 1921 they left the Village and went to live in Hawes Lane at number 41. Uncle Joe was the Blacksmith at the quarry. I spent many a happy hour leaning over the half door watching him at work. Seeing the horses brought in, and the old shoe removed. Scraping the hoof ready for the new shoe. The heat from the fire as the bellows were worked, the clang of the hammer as the hot iron was shaped on the anvil, and the sizzle when it was dipped into the water. I always shivered when the horse's foot was lifted and the hot shoe was nailed into place and the air was heavy with that queer indescribable smell. Not that the horses seemed to mind. Indeed, like us, they can't walk properly in ill-fitting shoes.

When the men came back from the forces they found things very different. Inflation had pushed up prices. Women had become more independent. Lots of women had been doing men's jobs while the men had been absent, and then, as now, we needed to export our goods. We can never prosper if our imports exceed our exports, but our prices had become too high, and gradually things got worse and worse as the expected trade boom failed to materialise. As the forces were de-mobbed the situation worsened. The housing situation was very bad in some parts of the country.

There was a General Election on the fourteenth December 1918. Women voted for the first time.

The next year, 1919, was a tremendous year for flying records. Hawker and Grieve flew from Newfoundland to Ireland across the Atlantic. Sir Ross Smith flew from England to Australia, Alcock and Brown flew non-stop Newfoundland to Ireland, and the British Airship R34 crossed the Atlantic. In November, the First Armistice Anniversary and Two Minutes Silence was observed.

When the Chaters left the Village in 1921 it was because they had purchased a house in Hawes Lane. Our new neighbours were Mr. and Mrs. Will Parsons and their little daughter Irene. Mr. Parsons was employed by our landlord, Mr. Williams. He owned the local Brewery, several Public Houses, and quite a few other properties. They were to be our neighbours until Mr. Williams had houses built at Belbroughton and moved from Siviter's Lane taking Mr. Parsons and his family with them.

Meanwhile other things of import had been taking place. Significant for the Midlands, Austin built his first 'Austin 7'. Marconi opened the first British broadcasting station, and gramophone discs were first electrically recorded. Charlie Chaplin made his famous film 'The Kid', and Howard Carter and Lord Caernarvon announced the discovery of the tomb of Tut-ankh-Amen at Luxor.

To a four year old life seemed very predictable. We had a comfortable home. Mom was of a new generation. No screens, we had a comfortable sofa. No large chest of drawers, Mom's pride and joy was an immense sideboard, it's mirrored back reaching almost to the ceiling. We had a plush tablecloth to cover the table when it was not being used for meals, and a large aspidistra in a china pot took pride of place in the centre. We had white damask cloths for meal times. I had an upholstered basket armchair in the inglenook, and we had several rugs on the floor.

Upstairs, in the very large front room, we had linoleum on the floor, and carpets by the beds. Mom and Dad had a brass-knobbed bedstead, and I had a three-quarter size bedstead which fitted into the recess. When they got married they had bought a light-oak bedroom suite. Mom also had a new Singer sewing machine. She was no dressmaker but she made pillowslips, and hemmed sheets and curtains, and made cushion covers.

Day followed day, and month followed month, with regular precision. Washing and ironing on Mondays, bedrooms on Tuesday mornings, then visit Aunt Polly or Mrs. Chater, Windows on Wednesday mornings, Sewing Class (later the Women's Own), on the afternoon, and so on all through the week. Mom's programme varied little. Every day had its set job and as nearly as possible this routine was never upset, well not until it came to Spring-cleaning time. What passes for spring cleaning today bears little relationship to the onslaught that spring cleaning meant sixty years ago.

Then, when the longer, lighter days of spring arrived, one by one, the housewives succumbed to spring fever, and everyone else in the family was expected to suffer from it too, at least in a mild form. Everything in the house from attic to cellar, had to be washed with soap and water, or a cleaning concoction of paraffin, or vinegar, brasso and such. All furniture had to be cleaned, then polished, and anything loose taken off to be washed. Rooms were tackled one at a time, starting at the top.

Drawers in dressing tables and chests of drawers were cleaned out and lined with fresh paper. Covers were put to wash, so were curtains and bed hangings. All the beds at that time boasted bed hangings. The beds themselves were high, with tall ends head and foot. Shiny black japanned iron with big brass knobs on the four corners and small ones in between, and fancy brass rails. Curtains were hung from the knobs down to the level of the mattress, and valences hung from the mattress down to the floor, all around the bed. So they all had to be changed. Any door having a glass panel, even cupboard doors, had little net, or muslin curtains fastened with coloured ribbons or silk tassels.

After stripping everything from the beds, dressing table and washstands, all the covers were taken down into the scullery and put to soak until the next day in soap suds left for that purpose in the maiding tub. Net or muslin curtains on their own in the rubbing tub, or a small bath. When all this had been done it was time for a quick cup of tea, then back upstairs to tackle the, bedroom.

We had a wooden tomato basket with a metal handle and Mom carried all the cleaning things about in this. Rags and dusters, paraffin, borax and water, ammonia, vinegar, and polish. Walls and ceilings were brushed, paintwork wiped down with borax and water, metal parts of the bed were cleaned with paraffin. Linoleum wiped over with a damp cloth to remove dust and stains, then cleaned with linseed oil to prevent cracking. Furniture was polished with a good beeswax polish. Finally the windows and mirrors, and the glass in picture frames, were cleaned with stale tea.

When everything was clean and bright, fresh bed hangings and curtains were hung and clean covers put on dressers and duchesse sets on dressing tables, crochet hair tidies would be hung from the mirrors, then a new mantel border would be fastened over the fireplace with big brass-headed tacks. Newly washed ornaments would be re-placed on the mantelshelf, jug and basin returned to the wash-stand, and dressing sets to the dressing table. Mats or rugs were laid beside the bed, and the room was done.

Then the housewife, dead tired, but full of virtue, could take herself off to bed, knowing that the whole process would be repeated each week until the whole house was thoroughly cleaned.

In the meantime at our house, Dad had filled the boiler with clean water, and when he got up next morning he would break the raker on the fire, and when it was burning brightly he would carry some through on a little shovel to start the fire going under the boiler. He did this every Monday morning too. This way the water was getting hot whilst Mom was getting dressed and having breakfast.

After breakfast the hard day's work would begin. Everything that had been soaking had to be put through the mangle and sorted into wet heaps, ready to be washed properly. The dusty smelling water was then thrown away, no simple task this either, the maiding tub had to be emptied by hand, first with a bucket, then a hand bowl, then finally man-handled outside to empty the remainder down the drain. Clean water from the boiler was then tipped into the tub ready for the proper wash to begin. When the whole lot had been rubbed, scrubbed, maided, mangled and put into the clothes basket, then the whole process had to be repeated for the rinsing. Eventually they were pegged out on the line to dry and hope there was no rain that day.

After dinner the usual day's work was usually done and then the washing had to be fetched in. Damp curtains and covers were rolled up and left in the clothes basket ready for ironing the next day.

When the weather was hot enough to take the eiderdowns off the beds they were taken downstairs to be thrown over the line to be brushed and beaten lightly to remove dust. They then had to be wiped over with salt or Fuller's earth to remove dirty marks, followed by a good sprinkling with powdered starch. Each eiderdown was then carefully wrapped in brown paper for a fortnight or so, so that the starch could dry-clean it. On a good dry day, not too windy, it was thrown over the clothesline outside and lightly tapped with a cane carpet beater to remove all the loose starch, before being packed away for the summer.

Witney blankets also were washed separately from the normal weekly wash. The water in the maiding tub was quite cool. Borax, dissolved in a large jug of hot water, was added to the suds. It softened the water and helped to bleach any stains. It was very heavy work. No matter how many times it was put through the mangle, a damp blanket was a weighty article to lift up on to the clothes line, and it could seem a tragedy if the line broke, or it came on to rain, and especially so on a shared yard where you could not depend on being able to use the clothes line next day.

Besides the mattress, beds had a bolster, pillows, and a shake-up bed, filled with either feathers, or flock. These too had their stuffing tipped out and the ticking washed. A friend, or a neighbour usually helped, especially when the stuffing was feathers. Doors and windows had to be kept closed, and hair tightly wrapped up because the slightest breeze and the feathers would flyaway, dancing like butterflies right up to the ceiling, and always choosing the most inaccessible places to settle afterwards. Then there was the whole process in reverse, getting all the stuffing back into the cases.

There were no patent cleaning aids then. On a shelf in the scullery we had various cocoa tins, and some bottles which held some of Mom's favourites:

Ammonia: For removing some kinds of stains, and removing moths from carpets. Cleaning coats and suits.
Borax: For softening water. Washing blankets. Removing some stains. Washing hair brushes. Cleaning drains and sinks and also as a mild disinfectant.
Fullers Earth: For dry cleaning. Removing grease from collars etc.
Paraffin, vinegar and cold tea were of course always readily available.

I for one, am more than pleased that we can take all our bulky bedclothes to the cleaners.

To return to the weekly routine, Saturday mornings of course Dad had to go to work, but later, often after an early tea, we all used to go to Blackheath. The shops were still open then and often we would see Uncle Tom and Dad would stop and chat to him and they would wait for the newsboys to come round selling the 'Sports Argus' and Mom and I would go shopping.

I don't think we needed anything in particular. It was just a steady walk after tea. We could get almost anything we needed in the Village; Hortons, Mrs Tromans, Miss. Good, Mrs. Oakley, and Mr. Aldridge, were all general stores. S. and E. Parkes and Hortons were Coal Merchants. Mr. Parkes and his daughter Lois. sold all kinds of Hardware and Paraffin in one shop and Drapery in the other. Hortons also sold Fried Fish and Chips in one shop and Dan Bennett, lower down the Village also sold Fish and Chips. His shop is still there. Fish and chips used to cost one penny for a fish and one penny for chips. Mr. Aldridge's shop was also the sub-Post Office. Albert Taylor was a butcher and I think Levetts also had a butchers shop too. Mr. Downing, Mrs. Taylors father, used to sell, Whitening, glass, putty and such. T.P.Moyle and Co. on the corner of the Village and Church Road, was almost like a supermarket.

Our grocery was always delivered. On Tuesday mornings Mr. Jess Howard, his shop used to be at the corner of Blackheath High street and

Holly Road, used to come for Mom's order. The groceries were delivered on Friday and paid for the next Tuesday when he came for the next order. There was no pay for bad weather in the building trade so when Dad had a good week, especially in the summer, Mom used to stock up with dry goods ready for the winter. Sugar, flour, dried fruit, dried peas, haricot beans and butter beans. By the end of the summer she used to like to see our big cupboard full.

If we had a bad winter I have seen the cupboard as bare as Mother Hubbards, but we never went without a meal. As Mom used to say, "God's good. If He can't come, He sends". She never wasted anything if she could help it, and she always believed in saving for a rainy day.

There were plenty of tradesmen too. We had a regular order for milk, and the milkman came to the door in his low milk float every day. He carried his churn and measures and you handed him a jug. The creamy milk was tipped into the jug from the half-pint, pint, or quart measure. The baker came every day too. We had Hopewells from Blackheath, and sometimes the bread was still warm. Now their carts were always high carts with very high wheels.

Several green grocers came on different days. Hobb's came round with hardware. The pots and pans clinking as they rattled passed.

Some of them would call to attract the attention of potential customers. Mr. Levett the Butcher used to call advertising his meat: "Roast, toast, baked, or boiled, Frizzled or fried."

Mr. Taylor used to shout: "Meat Buyer!" With a curious inflexion on the last syllable.

Mr. Moore, the Fishmonger would chant, "Herrings alive, six dead out of five, Two-eyed steaks sixteen ribs to the inch."

Joey "Line-Prop" so-called because that was what he shouted, also sold Bean and Pea sticks

We had our coal delivered by Billy Horton by the load. He brought it across Currall Road and tipped it by the back gate. A 'load' was a calculated ton. Could be slightly under or over, but you paid by the weight on the delivery note.

Then there was Sylvester. In the winter he sold Dried Herbs, in the Summer he came round selling sticky Fly Papers. He used to shout: "Catch yer flies, Catch em alive. Catch yer flies. All alive!"

It was not uncommon in the twenties to get hawkers knocking on the door. A lot of them were gypsies, but some were ex-servicemen, often limbless, selling sundries, boot and shoe laces, matches and the like.

Tibbett's sold Newspapers, toys, haberdashery, cigarettes and tobacco, and nearly everything else you can think of.

One thing I used to like to do if we went to Blackheath was to watch the men in the grocery shops. Butter used to be delivered to the shops in barrels and when they had to weigh up an order they used to shape it after the required weight had been cut, by using butter-pats. These were two pieces of wood like little bats. They used to pat the butter into an oblong shape before wrapping it in grease-proof paper. Very skilful some of the men were. Some shop imprinted a pattern on too.

After stopping to buy a few sweets from Sammy's (Mr. Adams) stall, and chat to anyone else we knew, we used to stroll back home again. I had to have a bath before I went to bed.

Sundays of course were very rigid. I was not allowed to play any games, or read non-religious books. I went to Sunday School morning and afternoon, and chapel with Mom and Dad at night. This was, I think, when I began to realise how important the Chapel was in our lives.

Irene (aged 4) with her mother

THE CHAPEL

In a small community, and especially in the days before radio and television, it was inevitable that the social life of the people should be tied up with the churches, chapels of various denominations, or the local public houses, of which there were many. Ours of course was tied up with the Wesleyan Methodist Chapel. Nearly every night there was something taking place. Prayer meetings, midweek service, choir practice, jubilee, mother's meeting or sewing class, later to be known as the Women's Own. Then there would be Trustee's Meetings, and various Committee meetings, or Concert Practice, and the like.

Meetings were sometimes called to discuss money-raising schemes. We were always needing money of course. Building Fund, Sunday School Treat, or Prizes, new Hymn Books, or Bibles, or the Heating and Lighting Systems. Garden Parties, or a Bazaar were as popular then as now, and many ingenious schemes were used to raise money. I remember one favourite way of doing this was for each 'Stall' to be allotted £1.00, after the manner of the Talents, then it was up to the stall-holders to use the money to increase his assets so that he could purchase all the goods required for his stall, and make a good profit on the day of the Bazaar. For instance, some made little lavender bags from scraps of silk, and sold them for one penny each. Some covered wooden coat-hangers, or embroidered handkerchiefs. Those who had sewing machines made pillowcases and bolster slips, cushion covers, and so on. Dad made toffee. Butter Toffee and Vinegar and Treacle Toffee. In case you would like to try them some time, I will tell you how:

Butter Toffee.

1 lb. Demerara Sugar
3 ozs. Butter
Pinch of Cream of Tartar Little
Lemon Juice.

Put the sugar and a little water into a saucepan, and stir over a gentle heat until the sugar dissolves. Then add a good pinch of Cream of Tartar, and boil until it will form a ball when a little is dropped into cold water. Add the butter, and continue to boil until the toffee is crisp. Then add the lemon juice, and pour on to a tin that has been well buttered. Leave to cool and set before breaking.

Vinegar and Treacle Toffee:

1 lb. Brown Plain Sugar
1 lb. Black Treacle
1 oz. Butter
1 Dessertspoon Vinegar.

Put the treacle into a saucepan with the sugar and butter and let it stand on a low heat until melted. Then stir until boiling, and boil until it breaks crisp when a little is tested in cold water. Flavour it with the vinegar and pour it on to an oiled tin. Break into pieces when cold.

These were very popular at school and we did roaring trade at a halfpenny a bag.

Then we had a 'Mile of Pennies'. These were long pieces of thin card with a dozen little pockets attached, each pocket able to hold one penny (old money). We all tried to see how many cards we could fill, but whether we ever collected enough to cover a mile I should very much doubt. Average one foot per sheet, it would take 5,280 sheets to the mile.

One thing we did not have were raffles. As Methodists, this constituted gambling; but we did have 'Guess the Weight of the Cake', 'How Many Marbles in the Jar', or' Guess the name of the Doll'. Of course not everyone kept a stall. We also had things like 'Hoop-La'. and 'Toss the Balls in the Bucket' and a 'Bran-Tub'. The ladies organised 'Refreshments'. A small section of the school-room was marked off for this purpose, and they were always kept busy. Plain Teas - Bread, Butter and Jam, or Fruit Teas - Bread and Butter, and a dish of Tinned Fruit and Cream. Cakes and Tea were provided in both instances.

Steam billowed out of the small kitchen every time anyone opened the door to carry in dirty crocks, or to bring clean ones out. Water was boiled in the big boiler, and a constant supply was needed for the everlasting washing-up. I should imagine that the steam penetrated through all their clothes; it's a wonder they never caught their death of cold.

On an Easter Monday we usually had a 'Tea and Concert'. Not much in the way of private transport then and so it was mostly local talent, but quite good for all that. Their repertoire was not too extensive so there did tend to be rather a sameness I suppose, not that we were critical. 'My Task', 'O Ruddier than the Cherry'. 'Come into the Garden Maud', Handel's 'Largo', and Beethoven's 'Minuet in G', and also very popular were songs like 'O Who Will o'er the downs so free, O who will with me ride', and 'Smilin' Through'. All of these were sung or played repeatedly, but they were good tunes and could stand the repetition. One trio I always liked myself was Ernie Brockhouse, Cecil Westwood, and Albert Taylor, all members of our own choir, singing a song, 'A Tall Wife, a Short Wife, No Wife at all for Me'. They all had good voices and I always thought it was hilarious.

Comedy was not well represented as you can see. Sometimes we had someone who could recite amusing monologues, like 'The Inventor's Wife', but it didn't always happen. It was usually singers or a violinist or such. Some of the older members of the congregation seemed to be under the impression that comedy was somehow sinful, but sometimes we did get a sketch played by some members that was very funny.

The one which stands out in my mind was called 'The Nigger Parliament'. I suppose it would be banned now and called 'racist'. A West End production could not have had more secret preparation than that sketch.

Dad had a silk Top Hat, and a frock-tailed coat, from his cousin. He had a large, very large, bow tie made from dark blue ribbon with a grey chalk stripe. The others also had large prominent ones in gay colours. I remember Ted Siviter with yellow spats, and the soles of his shoes flapping off. Old straw boaters with crowns that could be lifted like a lid. From the moment the curtain opened the audience simply roared. The setting was reasonable. The Chairman sat at a high desk, centre back, and all of the others were seated at low desks on either side of the stage, only they were not seated. they were lounging in all kinds of nonchalant poses. None of them had been able to learn the whole of their lines, and among the papers scattered about on the desks, each had his copy of the sketch. Neither could they imitate the American Negro voice properly, so they ended up speaking in good broad Black country, with frequent ad-libbing. I don't think any of the audience either knew or cared what the sketch was supposed to be about. The antics of the performers were such that any plot was superfluous. Everyone was too busy watching the little groups of players, afraid in case they missed anything on stage, to bother about a plot, besides with their faces blacked with greasepaint, it was very difficult recognising anyone, so everyone was playing games; trying to spot just who was who!

When the laughter had died away, following the end of the sketch. The curtains were opened to reveal a different scene. The men had re-grouped in the centre of the stage. Mr. Henry Jones, our organist began to play softly on the piano, and his son, Eddie, I think, had a ukulele, or a mandolin, I am not sure which, and they led the chorus in a medley .of Stephen Foster songs. It was a complete contrast, and very moving. The audience finally left to go home, some still humming, "Way down upon the Swanee River'.

Tailpiece

After the show on stage, another one began when the men began to try and remove the greasepaint, which they had never used before. I shouldn't think any of them had ever heard of cold cream. Soap and water was the standard stuff for cleaning in these parts, and the boiler had been left on to provide plenty of hot water. Wives and mothers stood around proffering advice to the men as they crowded into the tiny kitchen, trying to get white again. They were not very successful. Instead of black-faced coons, we now had all shades between black and tan, to say nothing of the striped ones where towels had managed to wipe off more colour in some parts than in others. Creases in the neck were very awkward. The waiting families were soon collapsed in heaps, laughing at the antics of the men trying to get clean.

Eventually, amidst much giggling, our patchwork parliament went home. The towels and shirts were never the same again.

THE CHARITY

As far as the children were concerned, the highlight of the year was the Sunday School Anniversary. Commonly known as the 'Charity'. I never did find out why this was so. I know Anniversaries still take place, but it is not the same. Perhaps because these days new clothes are not a rarity, whereas at one time it was one of the only times that the children had new dresses or suits.

I have heard Dad say that very often there was not enough room for all the children to go on the platform. The Sunday School then used to be pretty full, and families were much larger in those days, and so quite often, it was a case of one child from each family, usually one who could sing or recite well. Heaven above knows how some of the mothers of the larger families managed. Some of them paid a few coppers each week into a clothing club, but looking back now I wonder if they had many heart aches over the cost. Like mothers every-where they wanted the best for their children, all of them, not just the ones who were going on the platform, and even though they went without things for themselves, no one was going to have the chance to look askance at their children.

We used to practise after school on Sunday afternoon, and at least one night during the week. Mr. Albert Taylor, was the choirmaster for as long as I can remember, but we had different organists, all named Jones, but it is Henry that I remember best. I recall especially how he used to walk from Old Hill to come and play for us. We used to learn seven or eight hymns for the Morning and Evening Services, and a Service of Song, for the afternoon services. These were very popular at one time, probably still are in some places, and I think the ones that I remember best are 'Building a Church', 'Building a Lighthouse', and 'Signs and Symbols'. All the hymns and recitations carried the theme through, so some children had two recitations to learn, one for the morning and evening services, and one for the afternoon. Alice Horton was in charge of the recitations, and we used to go half an hour earlier than the rest of the children so that we could say our 'piece' before the singing practice began.

The week before the great day was always very busy. On the Monday night, the men would assemble to start the erection of the platform. Then on the Tuesday, to finish it off, and to test it for rough places, or nails that might be a bit jagged. Wednesday, the boards had to be scrubbed, and the chapel and schoolroom also. The pews and forms had to be polished. The drapes were washed and pressed, and fastened round the platform. Everything had to look spick and span. Thursday night we were 'tried out', graded like so may eggs, smallest at the front, tallest at the back, shuffling about where necessary, so that if two of the children had a dialogue, they were at opposite ends of the row, if possible. The tinies on the front row sometimes had a few lines to say, each one holding up a card with a letter on it. If they were not in the right order one tended to have an awful bit of spelling!

Saturday night we had our dress rehearsal, so to speak. Everything had to be practiced over and over again so that everyone knew exactly what to do next day. Walk on smartly, in turn. Stand patiently, without fidgeting, until everyone else was in place. Sit down quietly, when given the signal to do so. While we sang the hymns, Mr. Taylor and Mr. Jones would be listening carefully, to make sure that the sound was well balanced. Not too many loud singers on one side, and none on the other, and to make certain that the boys' deeper voices were evenly spread. Sometimes a final adjustment had to take place. There is much more work behind the scenes than most people realise. When finally, the rehearsal was over, everyone went home to prepare for the busy day ahead, and to get to bed early.

That was always the general idea. But, Saturday was not over yet. Back home, we had to have a bath. Very, very, few people had bathrooms in those days, so every family had to bath, or wash, as best as they were able. In a big zinc bath, or a little bath in the sink, or in front of the fire; the wash tub, the maiding tub, or even in the boiler itself, after the fire was put out I hasten to add. If none of these things were available, then it was a case of a big bowl, and a wash down as low as possible, then, put the bowl on the floor, and wash as high as possible.

The boys went to the barber for a short back and sides, and their hair was washed when they had a bath, but the girls! How they suffered. Hair shampooed, then dampened with sugar water, and twisted tightly round curling rags. They were most uncomfortable in bed. Bumps in all the wrong places, no wonder they say that pride must stand a pinch; - and if it rained, or even if it was just damp, no ringlets left after all that trouble, but, we still had a nice new hair-ribbon.

We always did hope for fine weather because of the 'walk-round'. This was popular at all the churches and chapels, not just ours. Some had a band to lead the parade, the Boy Scouts, Boy's Brigade, or Girl Guides, but we never did. Sometimes, if we were lucky, Mr George Aldridge came and played his concertina. He used to keep a sweet shop and the sub post office in the Village, next door to Granny Hodgett's house. He was a well known Evangelical preacher at one time. His playing used to make the hymns go with a swing when we stopped at the street corners.

Even children who were not on the platform used to come on the parade, after all it was their Sunday School Anniversary too, and we made a brave show when we set off in procession, dressed in our new finery. We did the Knowle and Tippity Green side the first week, so as not to clash with the Knowle Sunday School. Their first Sunday used to correspond with our second Sunday. Then the second week, we used to go through the Village, Bell End, Siviter's Lane, and finally, stop around the big lamp by Rowley Church. Everywhere we went, the people would come out on to their doorsteps to see us, and to listen to the singing. The men, and Dad was one of them, would go round with the collecting boxes, and the people would pop in a copper or two. I know of some years when the parade was rained off, when men, some of whom, would never have set foot inside a place of worship, have handed in a small amount as a donation, remarking, they had missed the children's hymns.

Back to the chapel we would march, ready for the morning service. Last minute panic prevailed as we were told the Order of Service. The children who had been chosen to say a recitation did a hasty rehearsal, some in a corner by themselves, others, to any friend who was kind enough to listen. It was always considered a bit of a disgrace to dry up, or 'break-down', as we called it.

This first service was always a quiet one. Never crowded, and usually, predominately men. Besides our own congregation, we would get visitors who had been pupils many years before. Often this was the only service they would attend here in a year. Through work, or marriage, they had moved away from the area, and some now attended other chapels, but, year after year, they turned up for the Anniversary, and if this proved impossible, would write, wishing us well, and enclosing a donation. How strong are the ties of childhood, they can draw you back, no matter how far away you go.

The afternoon Service of Song was a different matter altogether. Mothers and fathers, grannies and grand-dads, aunts and uncles, cousins and friends, all turned up to see the children. Then the chapel was packed to overflowing. Chairs were placed down the aisles, and anywhere else that a chair could be squeezed in. When our chairs were all used up, then we borrowed some from friends who lived in the nearby houses, Prospect Row, Happy Row, and the Club Buildings.

The children would file in out of the Sunday School, in neat rows. The little girls for the most part, in new dresses. At the morning service it was customary to wear last year's dress, if one had not out-grown it. We always seemed to have our new ones a size too large to allow for growing, so there was not any trouble usually, We wore little white cotton gloves, our collection, usually a threepenny bit, tucked safely inside, so that we did not lose it, and a few scented 'Phul Nana' cashews in a tiny paper bag, to be eaten discreetly during the sermon. It was the only time of the year when we had these scented cashews. I wonder who started it. Personally, I always associated peppermints with chapel. Mom always slipped one into my mouth when I was young to stop me from coughing during the sermon, so she said. That somehow gave me the idea that peppermints were a sort of religious sweet, only to be eaten in chapel. Sometimes of course, they were strictly necessary, there is nothing more distracting than a tickly cough, it sets everyone else coughing too.

Long sermons were not good for the children either. During the afternoon the Chairman's Remarks were quite short, and once the children had begun their part great concentration was needed to make sure that each child followed in the correct order. At the evening services however, I often used to think that the preacher was not suitable for Anniversary Services. In fact,

I used to wonder why they consented to come in the first place. They never gave a Children's Address, and often the sermon was not suitable for Anniversaries.

But, finally, on the second Sunday evening, the last recitation had been said, the solos, the dialogues, the anthems and duets, had all been sung, the child with the 'Begging piece' had winsomely made the final appeal, reminding friends of new hymn books and bibles, the Treat, and Sunday School Prizes, all needing money to foot the bill. The last collection would be made, and as the congregation sang the last hymn, the stewards would be in the vestry adding up the total collections and donations, to see whether we were up on last year's total or not. It was unthinkable that we should be 'down'. Outsiders tend to think that all churches and chapels have only one aim, the money in the collecting plate. This is not true. It is just unfortunate that the Expenses always seem to exceed the Income. Just like home in fact.

The Congregational Hymns were usually well known ones, and I used to love to hear them sung. There is something uplifting to the soul when a large body of people sing fit to raise the rafters. I remember four in particular, 'Summer Suns are Glowing', Pleasant are Thy courts above', 'Guide Me O Thou Great Jehovah', and 'Children of Jerusalem'.

When a pebble is thrown into a pond, the ripples move outwards until they reach the shore. So it is with sound waves. So maybe our 'Loud Hosannahs' are even now resounding away into outer space - into infinity - making a 'Joyful Noise Unto the Lord'.

THE TREAT

The other big event in the lives of the children was the Sunday School Treat. In the days just prior to World War Two, most of them took place at Whitsuntide. All the local churches took part, and with bands playing, banners flying, and floats laden with the smaller children, they would all converge in front of the sports pavilion in Britannia Park for a service. It was a brave sight at one time, but not so popular now.

Further back in time however, our Treat was held annually on August Bank Holiday Monday, when that day was the first Monday in the month, not the last. To qualify, a certain number of marks were required, and it was surprising how many tardy scholars returned to the flock, making sure that they were counted in the number for the great day. We used the field which was opposite to the chapel. The Grammar School is built on there now.

Everything was ordered the week before, and delivered on the Monday morning. Then the teachers, and the older scholars, began to work hard, slicing and buttering bread rolls. The big slabs of special Tea-Party cake had to be sliced and weighed, every child had to have just the right amount, there was no favouritism. The sweets too had to be weighed and put in little packets. Then the paper bags were prepared; a buttered roll, a raspberry bun with sticky sugar, a long iced roll, and the fruit cake. The bags were put into the baker's trays and counted, one for each scholar. When these were finished, plus one or two extra in case of emergency, then the rest of the rolls, and the loaves had to be prepared for the grown-ups, congregation and friends, who would have their tea in the school room later. They always had salmon sandwiches, and dishes of jam, and lovely shivering jellies too.

After dinner, the children would begin to arrive at the chapel. In ones and twos, in groups, and in families. Each child carrying its own mug or cup. The grass had been cut in the field, and the rough stubble tickled and poked at bare legs when we sat down, but the teachers and the older scholars soon had games organised when they arrived, sorting the children into different age groups. Soon the sound of happy infants chanting Ring 0' Roses, would blend in with the juniors singing Oranges and Lemons. The older boys and girls favoured Rounders, or Tag, some even practised running with their legs tied together, getting ready for the three-legged race. There was room for all to play in that field.

When the big urns had been filled with tea, all the children sat down on the grass. The teachers came round with the baker's trays all laden with the bags of food, and distributed them to the children. The ladies filled their jugs at the tea urns and passed amongst the children filling up their cups or mugs. Grace would be said by either Mr. Parkes or Mr. Baker, and then everybody could open up their bags and begin to eat. Food always tastes good out of doors, and everyone ate with relish. In these days of comparative plenty it is difficult to describe the days of deprivation, but a lot of the children, while not starving, were definitely undernourished, and yet they always seemed to leave some Tea-Party Cake to take home, remembering a Granny or Grandad, or even parents, who were not able to come themselves.

Parents and friends, and members of the Chapel, had been arriving at the schoolroom, and when the children had finished drinking tea, and had received their packet of sweets and gone off to play, they partook of a tea party themselves. Long trestle tables had been placed in two rows down the middle of the room, and the forms arranged around the table for seating.

Later they would all stream across the road and into the field. The bigger boys would obligingly carry over some spare forms or some chairs for the aged and infirm, and the children would stop playing games so that they could prepare for the big event, the Races. They were divided and sub-divided; by age, and by sex; by size and by ability. Sprints and relays, heats and finals. Wheelbarrow races, obstacle races, egg and spoon races, three-legged races, and team races. We cheered them all, winners and losers. The winners could go home happily, the few coppers which they had won were not to be sneezed at, it seemed like small fortune then. The losers, well they just hoped to do better next time.

As the day cooled off, and night time drew near, children and parents drifted homewards. Weather permitting, we always went across the fields to the top of Pennant Hill. At one time, in Haden Hill Park, there used to be a firework display on Bank Holiday Monday, and up on our hill we had a very good view. It was a fitting end to a glorious day.

HARVEST

Of all the Anniversaries, and of course there are several besides the Sunday School one, I always liked best the anniversary of harvest-time. One of the nicest times of the year.

The week before the Festival the tables were erected in front of our beautiful pulpit. It was such a pity I always thought, that the carvings of the bunches of grapes were hidden beneath the red plush cover, and it was so suitable for a harvest festival. An arch was built and fastened securely over the pulpit, and on Friday night and Saturday afternoon everybody who could, spent their time in decorating it. Masses of Michaelmas daises, Golden Rod, and Corn, were tied around the arch, and up the handrail on either side of the pulpit steps. White cloths were laid upon the tiered boards, and as the gifts arrived they were put into place.

Bunches of parsnips, carrots, leeks or beetroot, were festooned around each window, and small vases of flowers graced the window sills. Baskets of fruit, and baskets of eggs; dishes of assorted fruits, and dishes of fruits, assorted. Trays of grapes, plates of beans, the longest I have ever seen. Those who had gardens or allotments sent along their prime specimens of marrows, onions, turnips, and early swedes; and plates of well-scrubbed potatoes, just asking to be baked. Cabbages, green ones for boiling and red ones for pickling, and cauliflowers too. The grown-ups were kept busy as members of the church, and children from the Sunday School arrived to proffer their gifts.

Vases, jugs, even Jam-jars, would be filled with flowers, and interspersed between the fruit and vegetables. Everything had to be moved time and time again to accommodate another dish, or another plate, as the gifts continued to arrive. Then, right at the back, went the gifts from the local bakeries. Some bakers sent loaves baked like a sheaf of corn, or the five loaves and two fishes, as well as the more usual ones, which were oval and had a large crusty plait right down the centre. Then in the centre of the arch, a large bunch of black grapes was hung. Mr. Parkes always used to provide them when I was young, and they certainly looked delicious.

Early on Sunday morning, before the morning service began, any last minute items which had been brought, were placed on the tables, and then would be added a small lump of coal, a token offering for the bounty which lies beneath us, and upon which this community relied so much, and a glass of clear water, because without water there would not be any life, or any harvest.

'We plough the fields and scatter, the good seed on the land' every one sings with enthusiasm. 'Now the year is crowned with blessing, as we gather in the grain', looking at the loaded tables it was easy to sing of the valleys standing thick with corn, we had no farmers in our congregation, and as children we never gave a thought to either drought, or sudden storms, which may have ruined the crops.

On the Sunday afternoon there was always a special Service of Song given by the choir. Similar to the ones that the children did for the Sunday School Anniversary, but, instead of recitations, a story was used to link the special hymns. For this a reader was required, Miss, Gladys Robson, our local photographer from High Street, Blackheath, was the one I remember best. She read beautifully.

By the Sunday night, the smell of the apples and oranges, the plums and damsons, began to get a bit overpowering in the warmth of the chapel, tantalizing too.

There was generally a large congregation for the closing service, and it was always a pleasure to hear the singing, but I always liked it best if it closed with my favourite hymn, 'Hear us O Lord, from Heaven Thy Dwelling Place', by Thomas Henry Gill, and known as the Manx Fisherman's Hymn. The lovely words to this hymn cover all kinds of harvest, and always gave me great satisfaction, and yet, made me feel humble too.

Some churches and chapels have a Harvest Supper on the Monday night, but we never did. On that night we always had a Sale of Fruit and Vegetables. Armed with large shopping bags we made our way to chapel after tea to see what we could buy. People without a garden or allotment were always keen to buy the choice vegetables which had been on show. Some people had fruit trees too, and the big Bramley Apples were just the right size for apple dumplings. Sometimes there would be shallots to pickle, or a nice head of red cabbage. We never seemed to fail to fill our bags, and usually I walked home munching a sweet smelling Worcester Pearmain, which somebody had polished a rosy red.

As our Harvest Festival was early in September, even when the last bunch of flowers had been disposed of, it would be another month or so before the last of the harvest had been garnered, and we could presume to sing' All is safely gathered in.

ROWLEY CHURCH

When writing about the Village, it is impossible not to mention the Church. Who first decided a church should be built there is lost in the mists of time. As you travel around the countryside it does seem very strange that sometimes very large churches are built in very small hamlets, and one does wonder where the congregations for such places came from, and the money for their upkeep. Quite often they are in in-accessible places too.

Rowley Church, while not in a very accessible place, held a commanding position, built as it was on top of Rowley Hill. Not the Church which is standing there today, that is the fourth church to be built on this site, but the first church was erected in 1199. This church lasted the longest, until 1840. The second one, which was very ornate, served until 1900, and the third, from 1904 until 1913. The present church dates from 1923.

Although we were always associated with the Wesleyan Methodist Chapel, we did attend the Church on special occasions, mostly, weddings and funerals. As a child I thought it was immense. It could hold about a thousand people compared to our chapel's two hundred. I admired the pipe organ and the bells, but felt I would not like to attend church regularly because I always found the services too repetitive. The singing also seemed very restrained. We were used to singing with more feeling, or so it seemed to me. The prayers and collects, were, and still are, very beautiful to read, but it never felt the same somehow. We used to attend the services on special occasions from the Church of England School in Hawes Lane.

There will always be some mystery attached to the fire which destroyed the third church. No one will ever know the real truth of the matter I don't suppose, but I will tell you what Grandad told me.

On the evening of the eighteenth June 1913, Dad, Horace Portman, Fred Tibbetts, the younger brother of Ben Tibbetts, the barber, and another young man named Billy, were playing a desultory game of football in the mouth of Currall Road. Suddenly, they saw flames leaping up in that part of the Church where the organ is housed. within seconds, the flames shot straight up to the roof. The appliances were kept in the school yard in Hawes Lane, and the four of them ran for all they were worth, burst the lock on the gate and dragged out the equipment. They raced across the road to the top gate of the Church pulling the appliance. There they were told to go away as the Fire Brigade had been sent for!

Uncle Jack Guest, he was the Lamplighter, ran into his house, which was opposite Tibbetts's shop, and fetched a tool. He quickly, and quietly turned off the gas supply to the Church from the main supply pipe. This was in the street near to Currall Road.

By now, there was great pandemonium. Dad said he remembers Dr. Beasley running out of the Church carrying the Bible, and Benny Mac (Price) repeatedly calling out "Play on the bells, chaps". Hundreds of people arrived from all directions. The sky was alight with the blaze, and the

Church, a landmark for miles around, even in normal times, was seen like a flaming torch. Fire Brigades arrived on the scene eventually from Rowley, Oldbury, and even from Smethwick, but they were horse drawn in those days and the Church was burning fiercely long before they arrived on the scene. Uncle Jack turning off the main gas supply in all probability averted an explosion.

The suffragettes had been active in the outlying district, and it was perhaps inevitable that rumours would soon spread, laying the blame at their door. Dad never agreed with this. He said he never heard of the suffragettes burning churches, and he believed that it was an accident caused by some careless action.

CHRISTMAS

Christmas was a time to look forward to at the turn of the century just as it is today. It is not money, or the lack of it, which is important. Without radio or television, entertainment was found within the home circle, or with close friends.

Preparations were begun many weeks beforehand then, as now. Mincemeat was always made at home, and it would be packed into stone jars and sealed before being stored in the pantry. Plum puddings were mixed, with everyone doing their bit to help; scraping and shredding carrots, pealing and grating apples, washing currants and sultanas, washing raisins, the big juicy kind that had to be stoned and chopped, making breadcrumbs out of stale bread, prising the lumps of sugar out of the candied peel, and waiting for the lumps to be shared out, so that you could sit and suck it afterwards. Very bad for the teeth! Candied peel did not come in tiny pieces in a neat carton then, but as half oranges and lemons, much nicer than the new packed stuff. We chopped our own. Lumps of beef suet also had to be skinned and chopped along with dates and prunes which had been soaked in hot tea the night before and had the stones removed.

When it was all assembled and mixed together it was finally moistened, sometimes with old ale which was supposed to improve the flavour and keeping properties, and everybody had a stir. It was important to take your turn at stirring, for that was the time to make a wish, but you had to keep it a secret or it would not come true! Then when the mixture was ready, it was put into basins covered with greaseproof paper and rag covers tied on very firmly with string. The knots had to be really tight because if the string came undone the pudding mixture was lost, and it made an awful mess in the boiler.

The puddings were put in the boiler with plenty of water and the fire lit very early the next morning. All day the water hissed and bubbled, and the steam filled the scullery. The air was heavy with the smell of the old ale and the boiling fruit, and all the children from the neighbouring houses would come until all were sniffing the fragrant air and steam like so many Bisto Kids. If we were lucky, a little bit of pudding which had been boiled in a small basin would be opened and each of us would receive a little taste, commenting meanwhile on its worth, compared to last years, or perhaps some other previous year when it had been darker, sweeter, or as near perfection as it could possibly be.

Evenings had other pleasures. Christmas trees were not popular yet, nor even the Holly Bough, but the Christmas Bowl would be found in almost all the houses and this you had to make for yourselves, they were not to be bought.

To make them you needed two hoops from a butter barrel, some men were skilful and used three hoops. These were slipped inside one another to make a ball shape and where they crossed the pieces were secured with string. Paper strips were pasted around the hoops and then the whole thing was ready to be covered with pretty tissue paper. Long strips of this were cut and then creased down the middle lengthways. With some sharp scissors you cut the creased edge almost through to the cut edge, this was repeated at about a quarter-inch intervals to the end of the paper, looking something like a giant comb, turned right side out it was then attached to the hoops with a paste made with flour and water. The fringed ends made pretty loops and the finished Bowl in its many different colours was hung with pride on Christmas Eve. Any added trimmings usually took the form of sugar fancies.

Streamers for the house were usually Jacob's Ladders. Easily made with two narrow strips of coloured paper pinned at right angles to each other and then folded end over end until it was just a small square. The best of this, was that everybody could work on their own bit of streamer and then they could all be pinned together and you could make them as long as you liked, and of course, as wide or as narrow as you liked. Birdcages were very popular too, and again coloured tissue paper was used. Careful folding was necessary to make sure the centre of the paper was kept at the top, and then you folded it until you were left with a long pyramid shape, then you could begin to cut, snipping from either side alternately through almost the whole width of the paper. The whole thing was then carefully unfolded and turned inside out and cotton for hanging attached to the top. Good effects could be achieved by using two different colours one inside the other. Many, many happy evenings were spent making these decorations for Christmas. Dad says they hung up socks on Christmas Eve and opened them with joy the following morning. An apple, an orange, a sugar pig, perhaps a new penny wrapped in paper, a few nuts, occasionally maybe a new pair of socks or stockings, or a jersey, or perhaps a new pair of shoes; could be one small toy. A watch, a monkey up a stick, a Jew's Harp, or a mouth organ, small things that could be purchased from a market. Little girls may have found a little wooden Dutch doll with a small bundle of scraps for making dolls clothes. If there was no doll a wooden dolly peg could serve just as well.

By today's standards these little gifts sound very meagre, but that does not mean that they were deprived children. Children only feel deprived when they are treated more shabbily than their friends. When they all had similar articles there was no need for either envy or jealousy.

Dinner was of course an important part of the day. Lots of families kept a few fowl up the yard, or had relations who did. Some who had a pigsty kept a pig or two. Scrap food, vegetable peelings and the like was all used to make pig swill and arrangements made for a Christmas killing. A joint of pork and a cockerel were usually managed for the Christmas dinner. When this wasn't possible a joint of beef was bought for the occasion, in fact some people preferred it. Most people cooked the meat in front of the fire, using a meat jack. It was a long tiring job if it had to be turned by hand but some of them were clockwork, and once the clock was wound up would continue to turn until the clock wound down. A meat tin placed underneath the meat caught the gravy as it ran out of the meat and was used to baste the meat at intervals. Meat cooked this way was very tasty.

Vegetables, and the pudding, would be cooked in saucepans or pots, on top of the fire or hob. A contraption on hinges which were attached to the grate and was known as a gate, or crane, and it was fitted with pothooks, or gales as they were known in these parts. They were of varying lengths and were slid into position and allowed the pots to be swung over the end of the hob to simmer or over the top of the fire to boil. There was also a drop bar at the front of the fire upon which saucepans could be placed. Once everything was prepared it could be safely left while they went to chapel, then back home again to dish-up the dinner and all sit down together for this festive meal.

Afternoon and evening brought visits from married members of the family, and their children, also from aunts and uncles, cousins, in-laws and friends. A cup of tea, a slice of cake, or a mince pie, some preferred a glass of home-brewed ale, stout or porter then, when tongues began to loosen, chat and family news would pass from one group to another. Later, after tea proper, from a groaning table laden with all kinds of goodies, old and young alike would join together happily singing their favourite carols and hymns, sitting around the fire. I loved it when I was a child and our near neighbours came with their families, Ted and Mary Ann Siviter. We had an American organ and Sally, the daughter of Mrs Siviter by a previous marriage, played for us as we sang. Mrs. Siviter had a lovely voice and she always finished by singing At the feast of Belshazzer. Even now, after seventy years I can still hear her voice in my mind, such beautiful memories. Now all we seem to do is sit and watch television.

After the first World War a gradual change took place. In lots of homes now a Holly Bough began to be hung from the rafters, and little glass ornaments or painted wooden toys, sometimes home-made woollen golly-wogs, were joining the sugar pigs and sugar fancies as decorations. Real fir trees soon followed, sized according to how much you could afford to pay, and how long you could wait on Christmas Eve to see whether the price would drop at the last minute. It was supposed to be Prince Albert who first introduced this idea from Germany after his marriage to Queen Victoria.

Of course the shops were kept open then until all hours. If there was anything left to sell, and customers left to buy, then the shop was open. This seemed to apply any week not just at Christmas, or Christmas Eve. Of course these were only small shops and were mostly part of the shopkeepers home so there was no travelling to do when the shop finally closed. Tinsel began to festoon the boughs of the tree, and little tin clips to hold small fancy candles. These candles were usually lit on Christmas night for a little while, when we had our sing-song round the fire, and actually were a death trap. In the dry atmosphere of the home the trees dried out very quickly, and they flared up as soon as a naked flame touched them. It's nothing short of a miracle that half the population didn't get burned.

Artificial Christmas trees became popular with the families who could afford them. No pine needles to clear up, and once the initial payment was made it could be safely stowed away. Folded up and wrapped in brown paper, it took up very little room. All the little glass ornaments, and the other permanent decorations were all wrapped in tissue paper and stored for another year. A few new items added perhaps every year until a good selection was built up.

During the mid-twenties toys seemed to be getting more plentiful. Most children had a Christmas Club card and saved a copper or two regularly at the shop of their choice. With us that was next door at Tibbetts's. It was a double-fronted shop. One window displayed newspapers and magazines in the window-front screening the shop itself where the men and boys would be waiting for a hair-cut or a shave, because Ben Tibbetts was the local barber, and this being the age of the cut-throat razor, men preferred a professional to do it. The other window was broad, and it was usually crowded with toys. Scooters, doll's houses, forts, Meccano sets, Teddy bears, dolls of every size and description, toy gramophones, cricket bats, balls of all sizes and colours, doll's prams, magic lanterns, games and building bricks. We had never seen so many toys around here. Vaguely, I suppose, we knew that upper class children had toys better than ours, but on the whole we had enough, and after the first few hours of feeling possessive of our own toys were quite prepared to let someone else play with our mosaic if they would let us have a go with their stencil set. The anticipation however was more intense. Saturday mornings especially, the time when most children called at the shop clutching their Club Card and coppers. You would see them with noses pressed flat to the window pane as each child tried to decide what they would like to buy with the money they had saved, and voices would sometimes be raised in argument as they discussed the relative merits of the various articles on show. A little money had to go along way, and everyone wanted a good 'buy'. No-one could afford to make a bad bargain, so they clustered around the window changing their minds frequently as the articles which they had desired were declared rubbish by the older children.

Bags of marbles, dominoes, ludo, snakes and ladders, and draughts, were all popular, and were useful during the long winter evenings, especially where there were large families who could play together. Apart from Snap or Happy Families no Playing Cards were permitted in our house. As members of the Methodist Church Dad never allowed us to play with them. Scooters were perhaps the most popular of the bigger toys. Useful for running errands, especially if one had to go to Blackheath. Of course being a steep hill meant the last bit was a hard push back but it was well worth it for the speed you could get up going down hill. We thought we were going as fast as the wind. Incidentally, there were no brakes fitted to these scooters. The children who wore hob-nailed boots didn't do too badly but those of us who wore ordinary shoes were always in trouble for wearing out the soles of our shoes by scraping them along the ground, or the back wheel to slow down. Most fathers carried out their own shoe repairs on all but 'best' shoes. We had a contraption known as a 'foot', an angular piece of metal with a last for large, medium, and small sizes of shoe. Not many had a workman's bench but an old kitchen chair served the same purpose, and pieces of leather and tacks could be bought quite cheaply at Blackheath, also toe and heel tips, and hob-nails, for those who needed them.

Good dolls were not very numerous. Most had china faces and they had to be handled very carefully. The colour washed off, and the wigs came unglued, then the whole thing looked a sorry spectacle. If anyone did get one it was usually treated as a best doll. The kind to be looked at, wheeled out in a doll's pram, if you had one, but not to be played with in the ordinary sense of the word. no wonder the old rag doll, or jointed wooden Dutch doll were the best loved. They could be dressed and undressed to your heart's content with no fear of breakage.

By the end of the Twenties and early Thirties, and despite the continued hardships, long stockings were now hung up on Christmas Eve, and in the main they would be filled. Small things maybe, but filled nevertheless. We were lucky, we had a pillowcase to hang up. The few sweets had grown to boxes of chocolates and tins of toffees. The toy watch to real wrist watches. Instead of slate and slate pencils, a blackboard and easel with whole packets of chalks, plain white and coloured. No blue sugar paper to crayon now but drawing books, pencils, fountain pens, and boxes of paints. It was common place now to be taken to Birmingham to see Santa Claus at Lewis's, Grey's, the Beehive Warehouse, and other large stores, and to see the really wonderful Fairy Grottoes, and window displays. It was like being transported to Fairyland itself, and in our innocence we believed the whole world was now rich.

For one reason and another some Christmases stand out in our memory, and I suppose one of my first memories was early on in the Twenties. I must only have been four or five years of age. It was Christmas Day afternoon. We had eaten our dinner, a roast cockerel and a roast leg of pork, with all the trimmings, followed by Christmas pudding and custard. The table was cleared, the cloth removed, and the washing up all done. On the hob of the half-range grate the kettle was singing ready to make a cup of tea, when suddenly we heard carol singing outside. Two little boys were singing 'It came upon the midnight clear'. Dad said " Hark! Listen to them singing. That one child has a voice like an angel! He silently opened the door and I peeped out to see two very dirty little boys standing on our doorstep with a 'dobbin', a wooden soap box on wheels propped against the house. They finished the carol all through, then Dad smiled at them and invited them to come inside and sing to us again, They shyly stepped inside and sang to us again 'While shepherds watched' and 'Away in a manger'. Again they sang them all through. All children liked Dad, and he liked all children, and he could talk to them, and ask questions without giving offence. He talked now, and soon found out that they had been 'bat' picking, hence the dirty faces, because their dad was ill in bed and he had lost his job, and their Mom wasn't well either, she had recently had a new baby, and there was another child too, a little sister, nearly three years old. There was no fire, no coal left so they had gone up the Ramrod to pick 'bats' off the old pit mound. They hadn't had a proper dinner, they had decided to come to the top by Rowley Church and then down the Village carol singing, hoping to get a few pennies to take home to their Mom. While Dad was chatting to the children, Mom had poured them a cup of tea, and brought them some sandwiches. A brown paper carrier had appeared and food was being placed inside with a new loaf on top. Some coal and woods in another one. Dad promised to call and see their Mom and Dad the day after Boxing Day, with a promise of help. I knew he would, Dad was always ready to give a helping hand. In the meantime he gave the children three pennies each for singing, and an envelope with five shillings in it to take home to their Mom. The small shops would be open next day and she would be able to buy things. It doesn't sound much, but it was a quarter of a week's wage then. The older boy, he was around ten years of age, realised this and thanked Mom and Dad for their kindness. We stood on the step to watch them go. The coal and wood on the 'bats, the younger lad in the 'dobbin' nursing the food. We waved them off to Whiteheath, as they said, "It was downhill all the road".

They were still singing as they disappeared down the Village, the beautiful voices drifting back;

..And man at war with man hears not,
The love song which they bring,
O hush the noise ye men of strife,
And hear the angels sing.

Another year to remember happened a year or two later. Mom decided that for Christmas dinner, instead of the usual cockerel, we had better have a turkey. We had various members of the family coming after dinner, and probably friends too, so she wanted to be sure that she had enough for all for supper. To my mind, a turkey, which I had never seen, assumed gigantic proportions, about the size of an emu, I think, and I anticipated its arrival with a mixture of joy and trepidation. After much discussion, it was decided that as the oven in our half-range grate in our living room would not be big enough, and of course there would be a large leg of pork to cook too, the old baking oven in the scullery would be brought back into use. So Dad cleaned it out ready. Anticipation plays an important part in any preparations for Christmas and mine grew when I saw the size of the oven and I imagined it full of this mysterious bird, the Turkey, but I felt very deflated when I saw it after Uncle Jack Guest had plucked it and prepared it for cooking, although Mom assured me it was quite a big one.

Christmas morning Dad got up at 4:00 a.m. to get the fire going and the oven really hot. He got it hot all right - too hot. It must still have been too hot when he put in the turkey and the two legs of pork. One of ours and one belonging to Uncle Horace, Dad's older brother from down the road. The heat from the top of the oven lifted and burned the crackling on the pork, and the skin on the turkey was blown into blisters and burned black. Mom cried when she saw it- especially Uncle Horace's, visualising Aunt Mary Jane and all six children sitting waiting for a burned-up joint! However, Dad, disregarding Mom's "Oh dear, Sam, what are we going to do?" cries, proceeded to remove the burned crackling and skin. The meat was basted and finally returned to the oven which was now much cooler. Disaster was diverted, and the meat eventually was cooked to a turn.

Later came another Christmas memorable for a different reason. I had seen just what I wanted for Christmas right in the middle of Tibbetts's window, a fort. It was painted a mottled grey. It had battlements, a portcullis that could be raised or lowered at the base of the keep, and a working drawbridge over the moat. There were lead soldiers at the battlements wearing shiny red uniforms, and my fingers just itched to play with them. I handed over my Club card and placed my order, quite confident that Santa would deliver on Christmas Eve. Christmas morning arrived and with eager anticipation I viewed the assembled stocking and presents arranged on the floor. I looked everywhere for the large box I felt would be needed to hold my fort. I was bitterly disappointed that this one thing that I really wanted was not there. When I asked why Santa did not bring one, after all it was ordered and paid for, I was told that little girls did not have forts and soldiers. He kept them for little boys. He brought me other things, Annuals, and a toy sewing machine, so much more suitable for a little girl. I say he was sexist!

About 1927 we moved from next door to Tibbetts's to next door but one. Thinking of Dad roasting the turkey reminds me of the year he nearly roasted us. We called it the year of Dad's Yule Log. Like most women, Mom had a large mangle in the wash-house. The kind with big wooden rollers. One roller was wearing away on the inside, so a new one was obtained from Blackheath and one Saturday afternoon Dad took the mangle to pieces and replaced the old roller with the new one. After inspecting the worn roller, he declared it would make a good Yule log for Christmas night. He proceeded to fill in the hollow with wet coal slack, declining to cut it in half because he had measured it in the grate and it would fit comfortably in the half-range fireplace provided we kept the drop-bar up to hold it in place, and the fire wouldn't need to be made up again all night. So on Christmas day the slack was duly wetted again and the heavy log was manoeuvred into position. Early afternoon our guests arrived, Aunt Polly and Uncle Jack, Arthur and Jack Jr., with Aunt Sarah Ann from Stourport, along with Evelyn and Mark, and Aunt Martha and Emmie Baker. Eventually we all sat down to a very substantial Christmas Day tea, with salmon, home-boiled ham, pork-pie, pickles, fruit and cream, trifle, jelly, fancy cakes, Christmas Cake, and Yule Log, (the chocolate variety). As we steadfastly munched our way through this feast the log was gently steaming and spluttering away as the wet slack was drying out. Finally, tea was finished, the remains were tidied away, the washing-up completed, and we all turned our seats towards the fire. By now the log was smouldering no longer, but was crackling merrily away, and the heat was becoming more unbearable by the minute. It was a large room and we were all trying to move our chairs as far away as possible. The rear door opened on to a long hall leading to the back kitchen. This was propped open to absorb some of the heat. The front door opened directly on to the street, and when opened let in such a draught that the fire roared up the chimney like a thousand demons, but Dad had to pop out now and again to make sure the chimney had not set on fire. Fortunately he had swept it fairly recently. Eventually, our relations had to leave us, and finally Mom and I went upstairs to bed. Not Dad though. The fire still burned fiercely, it was impossible to put a raker on, so it was at least another two hours before it was safe to leave it banked up with a raker and wet slack, so Dad ended up Christmas by 'fire watching!' Dad used to do Fire watching during the war which brings to mind the Christmas in 1943.

One of Moms older sisters emigrated to America in 1912. Her husband had preceded her to find work and a home. In years to come their family grew to six daughters and a son. With the entry of America into the war following Pearl Harbour, in 1941, more and more American soldiers began to appear on our shores, including our cousin and 'cousins-in-law'.

At Christmas 1943, we heard that our cousin-in-law had a long pass for the holiday period and he was readily invited to come to spend Christmas with the family. He had stayed a few times before and we liked him very much. Food rationing made things very difficult but we did our very best to make everything as seasonable as possible.

On Christmas day, the table was laid and the dinner almost ready to dish up, when Pat, our Cocker Spaniel, began to bark and footsteps could be heard coming up the entry. We all stopped and looked at each other, consternation on every face. Who could be coming on such a day? And at such a time! I suppose we all suspected bad news.

I was nearest, so I went to open the entry door. Mom stood in the back kitchen doorway with a tea cloth in her hand, Dad had the carving knife and fork in his, he was slicing the pork. Imagine my surprise when I opened the door to see my cousin, Clarence standing there, smiling. He had learned that, Bill, his brother in law, was joining us for Christmas and had hurriedly applied for, and had got, a short pass and had hitch hiked and walked throughout the night all the way from 'somewhere in Scotland' to see him. It was the first time they had met in 2 years.

After the shock, everyone was trying to talk at once as we surrounded the two young men who were so ecstatically happy to see each other again after such a long time. We were all laughing and crying with joy as we were trying to ask questions and declaring it was a miracle that he had managed to get here at such short notice.

His great coat was taken away and a fresh place hurriedly prepared at the table. The food gradually disappeared but I don't think we realised what we were eating. Our hearts were too full and our emotions too charged to really taste the food. Our thoughts and our speech were very much with our relatives so far away, especially their wives and my Aunt.

Unlike today there was no quick communication with the outside world but we all said that if only they could know that the two were together, having a Christmas dinner with us, not in barracks or with strangers but by our own fireside and although they were far distant we were all part of an extended family and for just a little while that gap seemed very small.

Another memorable year came much later. I always think of it as my Rag Bag Christmas.

We found ourselves in the late fifties trying to manage on a very tight budget and I was busy thinking of ways and means of coping with Christmas presents when I thought of my ragbag.

Always being used to dressmaking I knew that I had lots of remnants and bits and bobs which could be used for aprons, cushions, padded coat hangers and such but it was my little daughter that I was mainly thinking of. Both children wanted a scooter and Martyn was easy, a few books and anything mechanical would please but Lesley only asked for her beloved doll Belinda to go to the Doll's hospital for a new wig and it was this that gave me a great idea.

During the daytime I carried on with my ordinary sewing but secretly at night whilst the children slept I made a complete wardrobe for the doll during its legitimate absence from home. Fleecy dressing gown, nightdresses, lace trimmed underwear, various dresses, a red coat with matching pleated skirt and white blouse. A dance dress in yellow net trimmed with silver beads, a raincoat and hood, slippers in various colours and pairs of white socks.

We couldn't get a wooden box but we found a suitable cardboard one and a long knitting needle made a rail. All the clothes were put on miniature hangers and hung in the 'wardrobe', the slippers in a row on the floor.

Christmas morning dawned, the scooter forgotten as Lesley sat entranced, gazing at Belinda resplendent with a new curly wig and wearing her new red coat and skirt. To see her face as she took out each little garment and replaced it on the rail was worth every hour that I had spent transforming the bits and bobs from my ragbag. (PS. She still has them.)

Most memorable, I would say, was Christmastime 1929. Granny Hodgetts had died in September and we were spending Christmas quietly that year. Aunt Polly and Uncle Jack, with Arthur, Jackie, and Howard, who was six months old then, had been to tea on Christmas Day, but on Boxing Day Mom didn't feel very well, so after tea Dad took me down the road to visit Aunt Mary Jane and Uncle Horace. I played at the back of the room with May and Doris and young Stanley. Granny Hadley was there too, and she and Aunt Mary Jane sat talking in low tones, while Dad chatted to Uncle Horace and Arthur. Dad slipped out later for a little while, returning shortly after to fetch me, and to announce that we were now four. Mom had had a baby girl. We named her Hilda.

A contemporary Christmas Card - looking up at Rowley Church

LEISURE

Much as been written about the Black Country, most of it disparaging. Well, I can't speak personally of the time prior to the twenties, but I can't see that we found it very black. Not Rowley anyway. We were told at school that this area in which we lived was known as the 'Black Country', but to us that simply implied a geographical name, like Blackpool, Blackheath, so Black Country, a name nothing more. The fact that we were supposed to be pitied because we lived there would, I am sure, have caused us much merriment.

Apart from the Village itself, we had great open spaces to play in. Pennant Hill, Hawes Hill, across Church Road, passed the Pound and Rowley Hall, the land spread out beyond the Ramrod pit, all the way to Whiteheath; all the area known to us as the "Quack", now the Newhall Road estate. Young children were not encouraged to play there because of the Quack Pool, scene of quite a few fatal accidents, but the older children went. Then away up Turner's Hill stretched the green of the Rowley Roughs. When we felt energetic we used to walk up Turner's Hill and come down Darby's Hill, Portway Hill now, then across Tippity Green and home. No, let other areas answer for themselves, but Rowley children had plenty of space to play games.

Traffic was lighter in those days. When we were told to 'mind the horses', it meant just that, quite literally. Of course we needed reminding. Although cars were few and far between, still a novelty in fact, horses were more numerous. Butchers, bakers, coal merchants, green grocers and hardware merchants all made their deliveries with horse-drawn carts, and there were governess carts too, and carriages.

Rowley Hill was a dreadful pull. A heavy load would often require several horses and they used to come up the hill with flanks steaming and much tossing of heads and jangling of harness as the drivers shouted encouragement from the pavement; cracking the whip too to show that they meant business. It was almost as bad when they came down though; with skids on, and brake applied, many horses looked pretty wild-eyed as they felt the weight of the load pushing against them too hard. So we did have to be careful crossing the road.

When the weather was wet we had to play indoors. Snakes and Ladders, Ludo, Dominoes, or Snap. Or we did some Girdling, with wool and four nails knocked into the top of an old cotton reel. I believe it is known as French Knitting now. I usually read a lot too. Come rain or shine I usually had a book close at hand.

We played outside when the weather was fine, often on the pavement. Hopscotch was a great favourite. Sometimes we marked the beds with chalk, but this could lead to a bit of a row. People used to sweep their own area of pavement every day and they disliked having it messed up, so if we used chalk we had to swill it off afterwards. It was much easier to use a broken knife, or a bit of thin stick, and cut into the dirt between the paving stones.

These were blue bricks about nine inches by four and a half inches, and a quick sweep with a semi bass broom soon cleaned them.

As the seasons rolled round, so the games changed; just as they always have. Hoops, or Bowls, whichever you wanted, to call them, it was often just the iron hoop off an old barrel' anyway, spinning Tops and Whips, we used to vie with each other for the most gaily coloured top, rings of coloured chalk and coloured tinfoil used to look very pretty as we sent them spinning along the pavement, but it was a hiding for sure if the Top stuck in the string of the whip and slaked off into somebody's window pane. We played Five Stones, or Jacks, as some people called" .often on the doorstep, and Tip-Cat, another game which needed great care. Some of the boys used to hit the 'Cat', a short piece of wood chamfered at each end, really hard with the bat, same with Rounders.

Cricket was usually played up somebody's yard so that the wicket could be chalked on the wall. Football never really died out, it was an any season sort of game. I think because most people, and the boys especially just like kicking a ball about. Mind you, a ball was often the one thing that nobody had. The ball was often a bundle of old paper, or rag, tied up with string. It served the same purpose.

On good windy days, in the right season, we used to go Kite Flying. We had a favourite place to go to for this purpose. Past Rowley Labour Club there used to be an old quarry hole, and beyond that a waste tip. The top of this made a rough-ridged plateau. The vegetation was sparse, mostly ragwort, coltsfoot and vetch, with small patches of trefoil and ox-eye daises, but in some of the little valleys, where the soil was a little better, there were carpets of soft green grass where we sometimes sat and played; but to fly our kites we used to go right to the farthest, highest end, there the air currents swept up the side and lifted our kites high.

As soon as the first one or two children appeared carrying a kite, there would be a mad rush to find suitable paper and string, and thin sticks, to start making one. Any newspapers left lying about would soon be transformed into tailing. Fathers and older brothers would be kept busy tying crossed sticks and pasting paper, then finally fixing the tailing. When at last, the balance was judged to be just right, off we would rush across Currall Road and up to the tip. If there was the right kind of breeze some of the children could start their kites as they ran passed the school wall, but most of us had to wait until we got to the top of the tip. Some of the older children were always willing to help the little ones to get started, then one by one, the assorted kites would go soaring off into the sky, spreading like a rash over the whole area.

We used to sit entranced on the edge of that tip, hauling away with our big ball of string feeling the tug as the kite rose higher and higher, dancing and bobbing, the tailing twisting and weaving as it played follow-my-leader to the acrobatic kite. Occasionally there would be a disaster as two kites became entangled and came crashing down, paper torn and sticks broken, the tailing dragging dejectedly across the low hedges and brambles, clinging to branches and thorns when only a few moments before it had been frisking about merrily in the sky, trying to make friends with the clouds.

For a brief moment we would watch as the unfortunate owners of the damaged kites rushed down the bank to salvage the precious string to use again on their next masterpiece, then hastily turn our attention back to our own kites in case the same accident befall us.

When the time came for us to set off for home, we would very reluctantly begin to re-wind the string, bringing the kite lower and lower until we could safely retrieve it, then carefully pulling the tailing over our aching arms, we would carry the kite home; hoping meanwhile, that to-morrow would be another breezy day.

Another outdoor pursuit we all seemed to enjoy, was skipping. A few children had a proper skipping rope with wooden handles, but these were usually only used if the child was playing alone, or perhaps running an errand, perhaps I should say skipping, an errand. For the most part we used a piece of old clothesline, or, better still, a long length of plaited fibre rope taken from around an orange box. Some greengrocers were very good and they would slip it off carefully so that we could make nice long ropes. These were very useful when a crowd of twenty or more played together. This was quite often the case, there were times even when nearly all the children in the street were playing together.

We had a skipping rope in our hands so often that it must have seemed sometimes that we were growing a new appendage. Year after year the old games, and the chants that went with them, were revived. In the playground during break, little groups would be playing together; Higher and Higher, by one group and Salt, Vinegar, Mustard Pepper, with the rope going faster and faster. Others would be chanting action rhymes:

> Teddy Bear, Teddy Bear, Turn right round,
> Teddy Bear Teddy Bear Touch the ground
> Teddy Bear, Teddy Bear, Show your toe,
> Teddy Bear, Teddy Bear, Out you go.

Or

> I am a Girl Guide dressed in Blue,
> These are the things I have to do,
> Salute to the King, Bow to the Queen, and
> Turn my back on the Kaiser.

This latter one must have been changed from something else during, or just after, the First World War, but I'm afraid I never thought to ask at the time what the original rhyme was.

All of these action songs were good for us, much more interesting than ordinary physical training. Sometimes, when a lot of us were playing together, we used to play games where we could change places in the rope quickly, so that everyone had a chance, or keeping the pot boiling as we used to say. Then we would play:

As I was in the kitchen, Doing a bit of stitching

In came the bogey man and scared me out

The next person in line ran in to be the bogey man until everyone had had the turn.

Then we had:

Cobbler, Cobbler, mend my shoe,
Give it a stitch and that will do,
Here a nail and there a prod,
And now my shoe is very well shod.

In this case, a new customer jumped into the rope, then they in turn became the cobbler.
To get several people involved all at the same time:

Mother, Mother I am sick, send for the doctor,
quick, quick, quick,
Here comes the doctor, Here comes the nurse,
Doctor, Doctor, I feel worse,
Then here comes the man with the big black hearse

Everybody ran out of the rope except the undertaker who stayed in the rope to become the patient, and the whole thing started all over again.

Then there was counting out. One person stayed in the rope counting the skips until they tripped up and were 'Out', and the next child started; or In and out, where you ran through the turning rope and out the other side. If you stopped the rope you were eliminated from the game, and the others carried on until only the winner was left.

Little groups in the playground could play either long or short games. Some were very long, and if the game was not finished it was not unknown for it to continue after school was over because they did take rather a long time, like this one:

Blackberry, strawberry, raspberry jam,
Tell me the name of your young man.

Call out all the boys names that you can think of until the girl trips.

Is he:

Tinker, Tailor, Soldier, Sailor,
Richman, Poor man, Beggar man, or thief.
When will the wedding be:
January, February, March, etc..
Will you be married in:
Silk, Satin. Muslin, Rags.
What will you drive in:
Coach, Carriage, Wheelbarrow, Muckcart.
What will you live in:
Mansion, palace, cottage, pigsty.
How many children will you have:
One, two, three, etc.

I never hear children playing these games now. I did hear some girls doing our old 'Teddy Bear' one, but they were saying 'Spanish Lady' instead. I suppose this is progress. We had scarcely heard of Spain, except for the Spanish Armada: and as for Double Dutch, this was skipping with two ropes turning in opposite directions. I don't think I have seen anyone skip that way since just before the Second World War.

During September, when the schools were closed for the long holiday, a few of the children went 'Hopping'. In fact, that break was known as the Hop-picking holiday. This was about the only kind of holiday that any of 'them had. None of us went to the seaside for a week. Trade was not too good, and besides, the children who took dinners to the local works had to take them during the school holidays as well. Some of the girls were baby-minders. For a small sum each week they used to help look after a neighbour's baby, or a toddler or two. Some had younger brothers and sisters and if they came out to play they brought them along too. Of course when there was a crowd they were killing two birds with one stone, because they could be playing, and everybody else was helping to mind the children.

We used to play at Hospitals, Doctors and Nurses, and we played Mothers and Fathers. If we could manage to borrow some grown-up clothes as well, we were as right as nine-pence. Strutting along Currall Road with oversize shoes and hats, pushing a doll's pram, was great fun.

Currall Road was a cul-de-sac as far as traffic was concerned, so it was usually quite safe to play. We used to squeeze between the railings and play in part of the old quarry. I think this must have been Church Hill Quarry where Uncle Jack Hodgetts worked, and Mr. Will Baker, Emmie's father. It closed down during the First World War. Currall, Martin and Lewis were the excavators, hence Currall Road. Our 'houses' were marked off on the ground with pieces of stone, old bricks, or, odd lumps of Rowley Rag. The game was played in all seriousness, as only children can. Doorways were left open and it was heaven help anyone who stepped over a wall to get into a 'house', instead of using a doorway.

Great ingenuity was used to furnish the houses out of any scraps that had been left lying about. We built fireplaces out of bricks, with red paper, or flowers to represent the fire. Old broken china represented money to spend in the 'shops'. Fine gravel made good sweets. Larger pebbles were joints of meat. Large coltsfoot leaves were plates, and big dock leaves could always be used as wrapping paper. Toy tea services, made of tin mostly, were useful for entertaining our guests to tea, only it was not often tea at all, but water. The railings were used for hanging clothes up, or hanging our pictures on.

Then, naturally, we had to have a school. One of the older girls would be the teacher. Sometimes we had chalk and a blackboard and easel, other times it would be pencil and paper, mostly paper that had already been used to wrap meat or groceries in, but it was in this way that lots of children first learned how to do pot hooks, or practice whatever it was they had been learning, whether it was sums, writing, girdling, or knitting. Some of the girls took pride in teaching their 'class' to do their lessons well. They told us fairy Tales, and they taught us Nursery Rhymes and action songs like Oranges and Lemons, Ring O' Roses, and Nuts and May. Sometimes tempers flared too, and everybody had fits of falling out with somebody, or even everybody, but, if their mothers kept out of things. and the wise ones did, everything soon blew over and everybody was friends again. It is very rare for children to bear malice.

Picnics were always popular. Everybody seems to enjoy eating out of doors and sometimes we would walk to Haden Hill Park. Bread and jam, a slice of cake, if any was left after Sunday tea, and a bottle of cold tea, home made lemonade, or just water. We always enjoyed it anyway. One of the attractions there was the lake. Not that that was our favourite stretch of water. We liked the canal towpath, or the canal bridge. The barges were gaily painted and quite numerous then, and as they came along we were always sure of a friendly grin and a wave of the hand, from the bargee and his family.

As we were playing with our skipping ropes and balls the boys would most likely be playing Ring Taw, or some other game of marbles. They got many a rap for having dirty knuckles through having played marbles on the way to school, or in the school playground. Nowadays boys don't seem to play marbles, there are no circles drawn on the ground, and no holes scraped out anywhere as there used to be. No singing as children used to do playing 'The Good Ship Sails on the Ally Ally 0', or shouting as they played 'Jack upon the Mop Stick', 'Two. Four, Six, Eight, All off again'.

When I was quite small and we lived opposite to Horton's Fish Shop, I used to watch the older children playing in the street, after I was supposed to be in bed. Street lighting was by gas in those days, and the lamps were set further apart than those of to-day, so each lamp formed its own little island of light, with dark shadows in between. But sometimes, that darkness was broken by tiny pinpoints of light, like a swarm of fireflies twisting and whirling about. It was the boys with fire cans. Any tin can would do. They knocked holes in it, and made a long handle from wire, and the sparks were caused by the lads swinging the cans round and round their heads, endeavouring to get the fire in the can to glow. Once it was all aglow it was easy to keep it going with the help of bits of coal, or even bats.

Other nights the street would echo to the shouts of 'Bedleyiron". I never knew what it meant, neither did I ever learn to play the game, but it sounded good. It seemed to be a similar kind of game to Hide and Seek. I could hear the call of whoever was 'On', Titimouse, Titimouse, Where are you?, and the answer would come from various hiding places, 'In my den, but not for you' and then the final cry of 'All up, All up', when the game was over. I know some of the grown-ups objected to this shouting in the street, but actually it wasn't very late, nobody kept late hours then because they had to be up early in the morning, and if anybody was out until about half-past ten, that was 'cat-squalin' time! I rather liked to hear it myself. It was somehow comforting to hear familiar voices calling out in the dark.

I wonder when was the last time I heard any children playing 'Queenie', or bouncing a ball upon the pavement as they chanted:

> One, Alaira, Two, Alaira, Three, Alaira, Four,
> Five, Alaira, Six, Alaira, Seven, Alaira, More.

Skillfully slipping a leg over the ball each time one said Alaira, and without missing a bounce.

When do they sit in grassy hollows rubbing the soft white coating from the centre of the coltsfoot leaves, to make 'photos', or carefully shred a broad blade of grass with a thorn from a hawthorn bush to decorate a vase of flowers. Do they still blow dandelion clocks, or sit and make daisy chains. Do they still play 'Picking petals off a Daisy', or hold a buttercup beneath their chin to see if they like butter. We did.

All this seems a long time ago, and yet so near. Our possessions may have seemed few, but we knew how to play and amuse ourselves.

I suppose it did rain at times, but like the sun dial, we only recall the sunny hours; but these were many.

PETS

When telling you my impressions of how we used to live, I cannot leave out our pets. We always seemed to have pets of one kind or another, although pet is not perhaps the right word for some of them. They were just animals, or birds, who were around the place, and they each had to be fed and watered. Dad was not overly sentimental about pets in general, but he did have an affinity with them. When we have been out on some of our long walks, the number of strange animals which have come to him never ceased to amaze me. Dogs with thorns or pine needles stuck in the pads of their paws, cats likewise who had small stones or pebbles wedged between their pads which they had been unable to move. Even horses, sometimes with only burrs stuck to their coats, all seemed to realise that here was someone who would be willing to stop and help.

He was used to having pets around. A cat for instance was a must. Mice abounded in plenty, without fridges, everyone depended on pantries and cellars. Houses were only lit by paraffin lamps and one usually took a candle if one had to go to the cellar. It is easy to understand how one could miss the odd mouse or two in the dark, especially since entry from the outside would be simple for mice, or even rats, through the outside grating which was used sometimes for tipping a load of coal into the cellar from the street. A good mouser then was essential.

Dad himself kept white mice. He used to let them run across a clothes line in the house, and when he went out he often took them with him in his pockets.

Grandad Hadley kept racing pigeons, and he had a dog who used to go to work with him. A good guard for tools and the like whilst he was working. The best one seems to have been one called Nettle. It was very sharp, and extra-ordinarily intelligent. It most certainly understood whatever Grandad said to it. Dad told me that if he went walking with Grandad and Nettle and they stopped by the side of some pool, a quick instruction when they came home, and Nettle was off like a flash, returning quietly some time later with one of the ducks. He could do this also with rabbits, but I imagine the rabbits were not always running about in the fields, but were laid out on an open-air stall somewhere, so perhaps the less said about this the better. With hungry mouths to feed, especially in winter when bricklaying was likely to be held up because of the weather, I daresay there was quite a bit of poaching done.

That the dog was cunning there can be no doubt. Gambling was rife in those days. Most of the men would lay a bet on any silly thing, even two matchsticks floating upon storm water running down the gutter. Grandad seems to have made full use of this knowledge. He would enter a public house with Nettle, and he would bet that it was fourteen inches high. Someone else would bet that it was fourteen and a half inches. When he was measured he would be found to be fourteen inches. Then Grandad would go to another public house, and there he would bet that the dog was fourteen and a half inches high. Now someone would bet that he was fourteen inches. This time when he was measured Nettle would be fourteen and a half inches. It seems to have been determined by the way the dog stood, but how did it know which way he was supposed to be standing?

As I have already said, they always had at least one cat, but the one that Dad remembers best was one which Granny had just prior to the First World War. It was a lovely cat, and Granny was very fond of it. stairs in those days were enclosed, and at the bottom of the staircase was a door. One night the stairs door was left ajar, and the cat slept on one of the lower steps. Uncle Wilf got up early to go to work, ran down the stairs in his stockinged feet, and in the dark, stepped on to the cat. He stumbled the rest of the way down, Dad following closely behind. When they fetched a light, they saw what had happened. The cat was dead, killed instantly when Uncle Wilf's weight ran on to it. They were both horror stricken. Not only because they liked the cat themselves, but they knew how much store Granny placed on it. Fortunately for them, the cat had died without making so much as a whimper, so after a hasty whispered conversation in the brew house, they took the body and hid it in the yard, and they hurried off to work. When they came home on the night, they took the body again from its hiding place and buried it. For weeks granny called Puss at the door, but right until her death in 1936 the two guilty culprits maintained a stony silence.

We had a roller canary in a cage. He used to trill merrily away on his perch. We were living in the house next door to Tibbett's shop at the time, and in common with lots of the other houses had big beams in the ceiling, and large hooks for hanging up sides of bacon, and hams. It was from one of these that the bird-cage hung. Now Mom was a great one for trying things out, and someone gave her a recipe, known as a receipt, in those days, for furniture polish. She put the ingredients, including beeswax, and turpentine, into the oven of our half-range grate. The oven must have been far too hot. So, not only did the ingredients melt, they must have boiled. They boiled over the top of the container, and running out of the oven on to the hot grate, burst into flames. The room soon filled with choking smoke. The poor canary dropped from his perch with a gentle thud. I was lying on the sofa having a nap. I was about three years old at the time, and this little thud was the last thing I heard before Mr. Siviter picked me up and ran with me outside. Fire extinguished, the mess cleaned up, and Mom never tried to make polish any more.

Dad kept racing pigeons too. I was too young at the time to remember them myself, but I've heard Mom speak of them often. If they failed to make the grade I understand Pigeon pie figured on the menu.

Like nearly everyone else, we also kept pigs. All kitchen waste went into the pig swill, and in turn, every part of the pig was, and in fact still is, used. It used to be said that everything was used except the squeal. I heard it said that someone at Marsh and Baxter's said they even used that, in the factory whistle. I'm glad that the killing is all done now at a slaughter house. I hated the days when the killing was done at home. I think most of the local butchers used to do killing. I can remember Mr. Taylor going to Stokes's carrying his big butcher's knives. I used to run and shut myself in the house, but it never shut out entirely the squeals of the unfortunate pig, or that of it's companions. I think they sensed death.

A rural looking Ross

After the pig was killed the hard work began. They had to be scalded and scraped, then cut up. If it was a 'bacon' pig, as opposed to a 'pork' pig, it had to be 'cured' It was then a long and difficult job I believe. Salt and salt petre had to be rubbed in by hand but nowadays fluid can be injected. The women had to render down the leaf to make lard. The best was put into a bowl and sprinkled with rosemary. This was lovely spread on new bread, or on hot toast, liberally sprinkled with salt and pepper. The trotters were cleaned, and then cooked slowly in a stew jar, and we always had them for supper, served with a generous helping of mushy peas. The blood mixed with some small pieces of fat, groats and onions, made black puddings. The cheeks made chawl, and the rest of the head made brawn. Intestines were washed, cleaned out with a cane, plaited and then boiled. These were chitterlings. Even the bladder could be washed clean and filled with the newly rendered lard, for storage in the pantry. There's no wonder that it is a popular animal.

I can't say now that I think that pigs are very endearing, though Dad said that I nursed many a tiny piglet when I was very young. Mom always said that this used to make her mad. She always kept me in white, and she had to bath and change me all over every time I went down to the pig-sty. Mind they do enjoy having their back scratched, and will shuffle, and wriggle, and squeal with delight, but they can also be very bad-tempered. This especially applies to sows when they have recently farrowed. Dad absent-mindedly walked into the open sty one day to start sweeping out, and the sow suddenly charged him. He didn't have time to open the gate again, he had to vault over the wall to avoid being pinned down. After she realised who the intruder was she was alright again, but Dad said he never made the same mistake again. He always made himself known before entering the sty.

Nothing to do with our pigs, but one day when we went on a trip to the country, we heard some pigs squealing and went to investigate. We arrived at a small orchard to find a herd of pigs quite literally drunk after eating windfall apples. I know pigs like apples and I couldn't see anything else about so I presumed it was the apples that caused it. I swear they were laughing. They were leaning against each other, squealing, and weaving tipsily about. Whatever caused the merriment, the pigs were really happy. It was one of the funniest sights I ever did see.

One of the funny things I wish I could remember is the episode with the goat. I have no idea at all why Mom and Dad needed a goat, but the very mention of the word goat always brought forth a welter of snorts and giggles. Mrs. Chater especially found it funny. The poor animal was fetched from Old Hill. It seems a brake was hired from Mr. Siviter, and Uncle Jack Southall was the driver. Mom and Dad, and Aunt Polly were in the back of the brake, and so was a basket of food. The goat did not take kindly to the journey and put up quite a struggle, finally doing something unmentionable in the basket of food, which all had to be thrown away. I have no idea how long we kept it, but I think I remember once hearing that Uncle Dick Hodgetts had it afterwards.

We also had fowls periodically. For a spell the conversation would dwell on the respective merits of White, or Black Leghorns, Buff Orpingtons, or Rhode Island Reds, or such like, and which were the best layers. I was never interested in fowls myself, but I liked the names of the breeds. I also liked eggs. Baked, boiled, or fried, scrambled or poached. I was, and still am for that matter, also fond of chicken dinners. So, I fetched the sharps, and the corn, from Moyles's. I helped Grandad dig the run over, and bury sunflower seeds for the hens to scratch for. We dangled cabbage stalks from the top of the pen, and we went across the fields to collect chickenweed for them, but I never had any affection for them. I found them nasty pecking things. They always seemed more interested in pecking my bare arms and legs than the food provided for them. I think they must have known that I didn't like them, they were always slower to leave their nesting boxes and go into the run for me than they ever were for Grandad, or Dad, and I would never have tried to take the eggs from the nesting boxes until I had shooed them all away and slid the trap door shut.

The chickens used to be pretty for a few days, and I used to like to see them dry out in a basket on the back of the hob. There have been times when we have had eggs with a particularly thick shell, and Dad has listened to the chick inside pecking away and gradually getting weaker and weaker. Then he gently lifted the egg out, and very, very carefully, made a hole in the shell for the chick to come through. I used to watch with bated breath, but he never failed to get the chick out alive, though sometimes it took an hour or two before they were anything like perky.

During one of the periods when the hen houses were empty we kept chinchilla rabbits. Again, they were for the table; and cooked in the stewjar with shin beef and vegetables, they made a tasty meal. Hilda was just a little toddler then, and knowing that we had some rabbits, Mrs. Rouse from across Currall Road, gave Hilda a big blue one. It had been one of Kenney's rabbits and they decided they didn't want it any more. It's name was Joey. Now this broke one of Dad's Golden Rules. He always told us we were never to give a pet name to a domestic animal, or when it is served up on the table everybody feels like a cannibal. Names create a personality, and believe me, that big blue rabbit was oozing with personality. For a start, it answered to its name as easily as any dog, and like a dog, it took to following me around, anywhere on the yard that is. Up on its hind legs, it would watch for me to come home from school. We had a postern gate in the wall at the back and when I unlatched the hen-house door it would come loping after me down the path to the back door. It was most polite. It never tried to come into the house, and it never caused any havoc amongst the lettuces in our small garden. It waited patiently by the dwarf wall for me to take my things in home, and while I took food and water for the other rabbits. He used to sit beside me when I cleaned out the other cages. Every now and again pushing his head through my arm. He really looked most peculiar with his ears pushed down. He liked having the top of his nose tickled too. I got used to having him around, he was soft and cuddly, and very affectionate.

All went well until Dad decided to get rid of the rabbits, and return to fowl-keeping. One by one, the chinchillas were killed, and eaten. Then came the fateful day when Dad killed Joey. Hilda came down the yard carrying Joey across her arms. His poor head shaking about, and his long ears flopping as she ran. I watched her coming, and for a moment, I was numb with horror until that second I had never thought to include Joey in with the rest of the rabbits. He was different. He was something special. I ran through the house calling to Mom, and she was as surprised as I was; she always said that if only Dad had spoken before he went out of the house, she would have told him that Joey was to be left alone. Man-like, Dad insisted that it would have been silly to have left just one rabbit, and carried on skinning and cleaning the rabbit same as usual. He jointed the frame and placed them in the stew-jar. We were all very quiet that night.

Saturday dinner-time the stew was ready to eat. I had been sniffing all morning. Mom started to cry when she lifted the lid. Hilda cried when she saw Mom crying. We refused any meat and only had vegetables. Dad carried on eating, stolidly and determinedly, declaring that it was the nicest rabbit that he had ever tasted. Supper time came and he ate some more. Sunday he was ill. We told him it served him right. He would never admit it, but we always maintained that even he ate the rabbit against his stomach. His own Golden Rule was correct. Never, ever, give a name to any bird or animal that is likely to be brought to table, unless, of course, you happen to have a very strong stomach.

Now cats and dogs we have had in profusion. Some of course stay in the memory more than others. I have no doubt that Dad would put Paddy, the big Irish Wolfhound, at the top of his list. He acted as nursemaid to me when I was small. He was gentle with us, and good-tempered. He would even give me rides upon his back, but if I went out to play, he soon growled if any stranger came near me, and soon put himself between us. When he developed a fatal disease and had to be put down, Dad was most upset.

Mom, on the other hand, always talked of the little black dog which Dad had bought her. I think it was a Pomeranian. When it was a few weeks old Dad had paid about fifty shillings for it, which was the equivalent to two weeks wages at that time. One day a gypsy lady came to the door, saw the dog, and wanted to buy it. Mom told her that the dog was not for sale. She returned that night with a man, Mom thought it was her husband, and they wanted to see Dad. Dad told them the same as Mom, that the dog was not for sale. Eventually they left, only to return again a few nights later, this time offering more money. Again Dad told them that he wanted to keep the dog, and it was not for sale. Then the gypsy lady flounced out, but she told Dad that if she couldn't have the dog, then nobody should. Mom was scared half out of her wits, especially when a week later the dog died, very suddenly. Dad said he must have picked up some rat poison, Mom said it was the Gypsy's Curse. I wouldn't like to say which it was. Coincidence, perhaps.

Of all the cats which we had, the sweetest natured must have been Tiddles. She was nothing remarkable as a kitten. A seemingly normal short-haired mixture of black, white, and tabby. It soon became obvious however, that something was not quite right. As she grew older, she stopped growing bigger, and she seemed more than a little pigeon-chested. She never grew bigger than a half-grown cat. Hilda was at the doll and pram stage at this time, and Tiddles just loved to join in. As soon as she could, when she heard the sound of the pram wheels, she would bound along and jump into the pram for a ride, with the doll, or without it. She didn't just curl up on the cushions, but would lie on her back, with her head on the pillow, and she would put her fore-paws on the apron just like a doll. She preened herself in doll's dresses, and loved to wear a bonnet, and when we laughed, then she laughed too. I never saw her claws, except to grip a chair cover, but never in anger, or spite. When Hilda told her to go to sleep, she would close her eyes, then, after a little while, she would slowly open one eye, and peep, just to see whether Hilda was still watching. If she was, she would close her eye again, but if she wasn't looking, then she would slowly turn her head to see if either of us were looking, and if we were, she would blink at us, suspiciously like a wink, then purring happily, she would snuggle down into the blanket. She was most extra-ordinary, and when she died she left a little gap in our lives that nothing could ever fill.

Some I remember for their beauty, like Fluff, the half-Persian. She was lovely, and she could have graced a chocolate box any day. Then there was Smudgie. He had a black smudge on the end of his pink nose. And there was Sammy, the jet black cat. We called him Sambo originally, but somehow Sammy seemed to fit him better. He went missing once. We couldn't find him anywhere, but one morning when Mom came in with the bucket, and a long handled shovel to clean out the grate, she had the fright of her life. She was kneeling down on the hearth, riddling the spent ash out of the grate, when suddenly there was a terrifying screech, and Sammy came hurtling out from underneath the grate. Mom screamed. The poker flew up into the air, and came crashing down again on to the empty bucket. Mom fell over sideways, scared to death by the black fury which she had barely been able to recognise as Sammy. He of course, had run like greased lightening into the brew house. Mad with terror, and screeching like a soul in torment. We hurried after him as fast as we could. For a moment we were afraid to touch him, as he spat at us with rage. We thought he may have gone demented, or something, but gradually, as I knelt before his hiding place under the mangle, my voice must gradually have reached him. His ears, which had been flattened close to his head, were slowly lifted, and he forced his poor trembling body to creep out towards me. Eventually I examined him to see whether he was injured or not. Surprisingly, he wasn't. His fur was singed, and he was very badly frightened, but no more than that. How he got into the flue, or how long he had been there, we shall never know, but if cats have nine lives, then I reckon he lost one at least that morning.

When you keep pets little mishaps are always likely to happen anyway. Heads stuck in tins, or bones wedged in throats. Dad always managed to get them free somehow, but at least he never had to remove a needle and thread from any of our cats, as he did for the pet cat .at the brickyard at Solihull. It was panic stations all round when he arrived for work that morning. The cat had somehow picked up and swallowed a needle threaded with cotton, and it was wedged firmly in its throat. Dad gently put his finger down its throat, and stretching the skin, slowly eased out the needle. He really was extremely patient.

The last cat which we had was called Nelson. Not that he was always called that. For years he was simply called 'Cat'. Like so many other cats which we had, he came as a stray. Being used to getting up early every day I used to wake up at the same time on Sundays, and if the weather was fine, I went for a walk. One Sunday morning, this cat, which was lying under a hedge, got up and began to follow me. I often wondered why cats decide to follow one person, rather than another. I know they are supposed to be psychic, so maybe they can see the ghosts of other cats who had followed the same person, and fared well.

He was footsore and weary, the pads hardened and split, and his coat was dull. We gave him some warm bread and milk; then he curled up and went to sleep. He was young, very large, the colour of marmalade, and beautifully marked. It was obvious that this was no ordinary stray alley cat, so I went round to the Police station to tell P.C. Huyton. Enquiries were made, but no one ever came forward to claim him, and we were afraid to give him a name in case he had to go home, or, as cats are very independent, we thought he might be a wanderer who would leave us of his own accord when he had had a good rest. We need not have worried. He had no intention of moving on anywhere.

As the days passed by, and his health slowly improved, it became even more obvious that he was a very handsome cat. The fine markings which began at the tip of his nose, fanned out across his broad head, down his back, and around his flanks. His manner was regal. His manners impeccable. He was house-trained, fastidiously clean, and very, very independent. No Tiddles here. He was not used to children, that was sure. He refused to play with Hilda. He would allow himself to be stroked. He would even purr, then, after little time, he would stretch himself, give an autocratic wave with his tail, and extricate himself.

We were all enchanted with him. Then, one Friday morning, Mom went out to the fishmonger, and fetched a silver hake. It was whole, complete with the head which she was going to offer to the cat. Our sinks were very large, and so she filled the small bath with water and immersed the fish until she was ready to clean it ready for our dinner. Before she had reached the door of the kitchen, she heard a splash, and when she turned round there was the cat in the bath. One flick with his paw and the hake was on the draining board. Mom hurried back and grabbed the fish. She was absolutely amazed. She had never known a cat before which had a liking for water, but here was a cat actually swimming. But more than that, she was shocked. The perfect cat was not so perfect after all. He was a thief!

Before the end of next week, we were to learn something else. Besides being able to catch mice and rats, and take fish out of water, he was adept at catching birds too, Large ones. (Neighbours Chickens!)

The following Easter week-end Hilda was very ill. She had Bronchitis, Pleurisy, and Congestion of the Lungs, all at the same time. Dr. Smith sent me to Bettinson's chemist shop at Blackheath, for the prescription. I had to go up the entry and tell Mr. Bettinson that it was urgent. The prescription was for anti-phlogestine, for poultices. The doctor called every day, sometimes twice, and everyone was very quiet. As so often happens at times such as this, everyone promises all kinds of things to the invalid, and Dad was no exception.

Hilda kept asking for a puppy, and for a budgerigar, and Dad told her that if she would hurry up and get better, then he would buy them for her. By now, it was high summer, and everywhere we enquired we were told that it was not the right time of the year. Poor Mom was worried stiff, what with Hilda being ill, and wondering how on earth she was going to manage with a sick child, a puppy, a bird, and a cat who caught and eat birds as though he had a divine right.

The weeks went slowly by, then, just when she thought she was going to be let off, cousin Dennis Wroe brought a green budgie from someone at Halesowen. Ordinarily it would not have been for sale. It was about a year old, and it had been living in an aviary with canaries. He sold it to Dennis after hearing how sick Hilda was. The budgie in his new cage pacified her until she was able to get up. Dennis was very tall, and was nicknamed Tiny. It was decided to call the bird Tiny also.

We were very friendly with P.C. Huyton and Mrs. Huyton, and when he was on the beat Mr. Huyton listened out for news of any puppies for sale. Eventually he heard of some people who bred spaniels, and red setters. A spaniel bitch had just had a litter of pups. They were not pure bred, but what is known as first-cross. In other words they were mixed spaniel and setter, and they had one puppy left, a bitch. Dad decided to have it, so eventually Mr. Huyton delivered to us one little ball of liver and white wool that squirmed all over the place, and Hilda called her Pat.

So now we were a three pet family, and our fun began. Right from the start each one was jealous of the other two. Young though she was, especially in the case of the cat, Pat realised that she had to vie for our affection. The cat treated the puppy with disdain, especially when she yelped in the night, but Tiny was different. Knowing his habit of stalking, and killing, even big birds, we all tried to protect the budgie from the cat. We had a Singer treadle sewing machine, the kind that drops inside making a flat table top. It stood in front of the window, and was ideal for the budgie's cage. We came in once to find the cat had just jumped up on to the end of the table and was watching the bird through narrowed eyes. Dad took a hurried step forward and, for the first and only time, hit him. The cat fled outside and sulked; but he never again sat by the side of the cage. Dad had been afraid that Tiny might have been scared to death, but I think Tiny understood very well that as long as he was in the cage, he was quite safe.

Actually, we did understand how the poor cat must feel. From being the centre of attention, which suited his ego very well, he suddenly found two rivals had appeared upon the scene, and they must have seemed to be getting more attention than he was. As they all grew older however, they became a little more amicable, always providing each one felt he was getting his fair share of affection, and of anything else that was going. Pets can be great tyrants.

Tiny liked a drop of tea, so Pat and the cat had to have a drink of tea. If Pat had a dog biscuit, then the cat had to have a morsel of something, and Tiny rattled his cage until we at least made a pretence of putting him a little birdseed. If he was out of the cage, he would run races up and down your back to make you bend down to the cupboard where his seed tin was kept.'

He wasn't averse to tweaking the hair at the nape of your neck, or even the end of your ear, if he wanted to draw attention to himself. On Saturdays I bought Tiny a millet spray in a paper bag. He used to try to get into my pocket if I didn't give it to him immediately, then Pat and the cat had to have a chocolate drop, just to keep the peace. Who says they are dumb animals?

During the dark days of the War we still managed to feed them. The cat used to sit on the wall waiting for the fishmonger. Kneading his paws, and purring in anticipation of one or two succulent fish heads, and an occasional herring, if he was lucky. Pat ate the household scraps, a few bits from the butcher and a bone besides, and the usual dog-biscuits. The birdseed got more difficult but we managed.

While the War was raging on the continent, we had our own battles going on, this time on our own backyard. Mrs. Clifford, our next door neighbour, had a tabby cat, another tom, and Aunt Polly, next door but one, acquired a she-cat. War was declared with a vengeance. Many a battle royal took place with fur flying in all directions. They would sometimes sit for hours staring at one another from opposite ends of the dividing wall. Occasionally spitting and swearing at one another, and gradually creeping nearer and nearer to each other, then when they were within paw distance the skirmish would start in earnest. One unfortunate day the battle became more fierce, and as our cat reached out with his long forepaw and savagely clawed the neck of the Tabby, so tabby's shorter paw reached his rival's eye. Both screamed with pain and rage. The battle forgotten for the moment as each jumped down from the wall to their respective back-yards, and ran off to nurse their wounds. Next door tabby had a terribly long scratch almost half-way round his neck. It bled profusely for a little while, but later he was as good as new. Our cat hid himself away for days. When we saw him again we realised he had been injured more than we had thought. He was now blind in his left eye. We never called him 'the cat' again. Now he was Nelson.

We had trouble with Pat also. One Monday morning when Mom was preparing to do the weekly wash, she discovered a stub of indelible pencil in Hilda's pocket. She had just left school and had started to work at the Co-operative shop in Hawes Lane. Mom took the pencil out, but she must have dropped it on the floor. Pat found it and decided it must be something to eat. She went purple right through from mouth to tail. Dad said she was poisoned and would have to be put down. We cried and we pleaded for time. For two weeks she lay in her box like a stone. Only her eyes told us that she was still alive. The poison was doing its deadly work.

Every hour of the day, and night too, we dribbled a little fluid into her mouth, and with a bit of rag I cleaned her teeth and the inside of her mouth. Eventually Dad said we were being cruel trying to keep her alive, even though she was not in any pain, and he said that when he came home on the Saturday afternoon, she would definitely have to go. Saturday morning dawned, and I ran downstairs to Pat, and to inspect her in broad daylight. Lo and behold! There was a small miracle. Two front teeth and the tip of her tongue were clear of the deadly blue poison. We waited with bated breath for Dad to come home from work. He knelt down beside her box and gently prised open her mouth to inspect her teeth and tongue. Pat opened her eyes and looked at him, and her tail gave a tiny flicker, and I knew then that we had won. Such love and trust in a dog's eyes cannot be betrayed. Dad rose to his feet, agreeing very gruffly, that we could try for a few more days.

She began to mend very slowly, and I think we all wondered sometimes whether we ought to have let her go, but as the weather improved, so did Pat. As soon as she was able to take solid food again she picked up by leaps and bounds, and before Autumn came she was frolicking about, her ears flopping about everywhere, just like before.

For the next two years, everything carried on normally, then one Sunday morning I cleaned out Tiny's cage, and I put in a new sand sheet, refilled his seed trough, and washed out and cleaned his water trough. He had had his little fly around, and then he settled on the window sash and watched all that I was doing, and, when I had finished I left open the door of his cage, and in he flew, straight to his seed trough and nibbled away for a little time. Because I had a friend staying with me for the week-end who was not used to having a bird flying about, I shut the door of the cage. I need not have bothered. A few seconds later Tiny fell from his perch on to the floor of his cage. He was dead. To say that we were shocked is putting it mildly. It was so quick that we all felt stupefied. We put his little body into a cocoa tin and buried it in the garden.

We all missed him very much. We missed his ceaseless chatter, and we missed his tuneful whistling, especially when a brass band played on the wireless. He always loved a brass band. But most of all we missed his little pranks. Hiding behind the big mirror when he saw us getting ready to go out, or worse still, behind the plant pots high up in the verandah. By the time you had fetched something to stand on he had flown away to a fresh vantage place. Then there were times when he sat on top of his cage chattering derisively at Nelson as he sat on the windowsill outside, tapping the glass to attract our attention, and let him in. The more he tapped, the more Tiny would chatter, mocking the cat's discomfiture, more so if it was raining. I've seen him sitting there with his ears flattened, and his eyes narrowed, and I think he could quite cheerfully have killed Tiny if he could, but, when we let him in, he would run to his usual spot on the hearth, and turn his back on Tiny. Now he just kept looking at the empty place, and miaowed plaintively. Aware from our attitude that there was something wrong, but perhaps not sure exactly what it was.

Only a few months afterwards, Nelson himself, failed to come home on the Saturday morning. We were not worried at all about this. Cats own you. Nobody owns a cat. They come and go as they please. When however, he had not come home on Sunday morning, we did begin to wonder what had become of him. He was beginning to get old now. He was fully grown when he came to us. Young, we could see, but not how young, and, since losing the sight of one eye, we knew he was more vulnerable. We were just putting on our coats to go to chapel, and Dad was just about to have his dinner. He had had to go to work that day to do some maintenance job, when we heard a slight sound in the entry. I rushed to open the entry door, and the sight which met our eyes was enough to turn anyone's heart over. Our once beautiful, regal, independent cat, was lying across the threshold miaowing weakly and piteously. Where-ever he had been, he had been tied up, the fur around his neck was rubbed away, showing how much he had struggled. Worse he had been badly beaten, hit so severely over the head that he was now completely blind. How he had managed to crawl home, we couldn't guess, some feline instinct, I suppose. He lifted up his head a little when he heard our voices, then he sank back on to the floor of the verandah. He had come back home, only to die just as he had reached safety. We were all grieved. We would have wished for him a much easier passing.

We were back now to a one pet family. After all the years of being extra careful, not to leave any food lying about, or not to show more attention to one pet than to the other two, it did seem very strange.

We were to have Pat for another five years. She went with Blackie, Aunt Polly's spaniel into the valley at the' back. The gas men had the road up at the corner of Hawes Lane and Giles Avenue and the dogs ran out into the road to get round the workings. Pat was hit by a passing car, and killed outright. As I write this, thirty five years have gone by, and yet, sometimes when I am sitting quietly, either reading or watching Television, I suddenly feel my knee grow warm, and I put out my hand to stroke Pat's head. I can never believe that she isn't there.

TRAVEL

I suppose we all at sometime in our lives get the urge to travel, as the song says 'To far away places with strange sounding names'. Learning the poem 'Cargoes' by John Masefield, was I think the starting point for me. It embodied the fabulous journey of the Queen of Sheba to visit King Solomon, Francis Drake and Walter Raleigh and the mysterious El Dorado, Casablanca, Tristan da Cunha, and the Golden Road to Samarkand. All names to fire the imagination, and to give the toes a magic carpet twitch; and sixty years ago we stood as much chance of getting a magic carpet as we stood of visiting these romantic sounding places.

Today's magic carpet is the jet plane. To fly abroad now is commonplace. With an early start it is quite possible to go to Paris, Amsterdam, or further afield, spend some eight hours there before the flight back, and still be home before midnight. Flying with Concorde it is even possible to fly to New York and back in one day.

Because of its geographical position, Rowley Village was a bit of an island as far as public transport was concerned. Stage coaches used to run regularly from Dudley, from Wolverhampton, and from Birmingham. The London stage coaches used to call at Wednesbury even, on their way to the North. The coming of the railways opened up the country, and for the first time ordinary people were given the chance to go to the sea-side or country in comparative ease, mainly by taking advantage of excursion trains. The railways people had soon discovered that it is better to carry a full train load at cheap rates than to try to carry a few people at full fare. (I think we could have done with a few of these far seeing men about again before Dr. Beeching got busy with his big axe) Even so, Rowley Regis and Blackheath station is not very conveniently sited. It was not possible to catch a bus to the station. Whether this was a deliberate policy on the side of the Midland Red, so as not to make things easy for a rival company, I can't say, or it may have been the local councillors who never made any effort to correct this.

Blackheath fared better when the tramcars came. There were services to Oldbury, and to Old Hill and Cradley Heath. From Old Hill it was possible to catch a tram to Dudley, via Netherton, and Dudley itself was quite well served. Rowley Hill being very steep excluded any tramcar service from Birmingham to Dudley via Blackheath, this had to wait until the Midland Red buses began to run. On this route too there was another nasty bit of road. On the New Rowley Road, travelling from the Royal Oak towards Dudley, the road was subject to subsidence owing to the local pit workings, and from the Cross Keys, where now it is a gently incline, was a steep piece known as Carlyle Hill. If you look closely you will be able to see where this hill was lowered, leaving the existing properties way above the new level, and now they have a gate in the wall, and a flight of steps to reach their front doors.

The roads then were not tarmaced like ours are to-day. They were tarred and metalled, but the stones were not finely cut, but were left in a rough state. They were also very dusty. To help lay the dust the council watering cart came round at intervals. This was horse drawn and carried a water tank on the cart, a pipe along the back had two rows of holes through which the water spurted, to the great delight of the children, and the cart would go up one side of the road, and down the other. It was a full time job.

The better-off families might have a pony and trap, or a governess cart, and richer people had their own carriages. Just a few of the larger houses had stables and carriage houses, later to be turned into garages when motor cars became fashionable. There were a few bicycles about, the old 'sit up and beg' type, which must have shaken you to pieces on those rough roads. Not many people could afford these however, so mostly the common form of transport was one's own legs. Money was needed desperately for necessities, not fares. As I have said elsewhere, Granny Hadley told me how they used to walk to Birmingham to do special shopping, and my father-in-Law walked alone from somewhere near Swansea when he was 'quite a young lad because there was no work available in South Wales.

Naturally, nearly everyone worked near to their home, the quarries, local pits, T.W. Lench Ltd., and lots of small industries which had sprung up locally. In this way time was not wasted in travelling, but the actual hours worked in those days was much longer than to-day, no forty hour weeks then. Despite this, they were still willing to go out again later, sometimes only to their favourite public house, but the churches and chapels were always well represented too and special services held in places outside the area, Dudley, Blackheath, Oldbury, Old Hill and Cradley Heath, always drew a good percentage of hardy souls who were prepared to walk from the Village, and walk back too.

Week-ends too meant walking. Some of the young men belonged to Football Clubs. Nearly every church or chapel could boast its own team. Remember that some of the famous Clubs started out as Sunday School teams. We had one at Hawes Lane and I have heard Dad say that he has played in Charity matches where everyone, players, linesmen, and the referee, have all been named Hadley. Imagine having to commentate at that one! In most cases they had been to work, then walked to the ground, played in the match, and then walked home again.

Walking for pleasure was very satisfying however, no matter what time of the year it was. I have walked with Dad for miles and miles. Of course it was all open then. No housing schemes had been built. We used to walk up Turner's Hill, and always we stopped to admire the view. I remember how I always wished I could go into the house which later became the A.R.C. offices, (now demolished), because I always thought how good their views must be. From there we had a choice. We could turn left across the golf links and come out down the Knowle, the footpath brings you out by the Hailstone Inn, or we could carry on to the Wheatsheaf, turn left there, down Oakham road, to Dixon's Green and New Rowley Road, or cut down the footpath at Warren's Hall Farm and come out by the Royal Oak. If the weather was very nice, we sometimes crossed over the road at the Wheatsheaf and went down Gypsy Lane, now called

City Road, and carryon along what is now the new Wolverhampton Road as far as Newbury Lane, and back to Portway and Tippity Green, and of course from the Wheatsheaf there was the right turn down Darby's Hill, now called Portway Hill, but that was a short walk.

These walks, so very near to home, were then like country lanes. No footpaths, the hedgerows grew right up to the edge of the road in most places. In the Spring the scent of the may blossom was almost overpowering. We have walked across the canal towpath at Titford and it was like stepping into another world. with the water on one side and the white blossom weighing down the branches on the other; blue sky overhead, swans swimming near to the trees on the farther bank and skylarks soaring, higher and higher, their song getting ever more sweet. Sometimes it seemed almost too much to bear. We have stood to listen and my heart would swell until my chest seemed ready to burst, my throat felt dry, and I could have wept, but I didn't quite know why.

The landscape changed with the seasons here as elsewhere. Spring gave way to Summer. The soft green leaves on the trees grew bigger and darker, and every day the outline of the branches became hidden a little more. The may blossom shrivelled and died, and when you looked closely the tiny round shape of the berry could be seen forming. Hedgerows and fields were crowded with flowers. Buttercups and daises, speedwell and clover, lady's smocks and cross irons. Mallow, trefoil, coltsfoot, ragwort, vetch and dandelion, tall cow parsley, climbing convolvulous, and dainty ladies lace. We used to collect them and press them in books; take them to school to stand in jam jars on window sills and cupboards. pit mound and quarry tip, each had a share of hardy tufts of coarse grass, ox-eye daises, yarrow and toadflax.

With horses as the main means of transport, many of the fields were given over each year to growing grass for feeding these, and cows. It was always known then as ' mowing grass'. When it grew tall it was like watching a sheet of water. The breeze swayed the grass in long waves making an ever-changing pattern of light and shade, and we were always being told to keep to the paths and not tread down the grass. It was mostly hand scythed in those days and flattened grass was more difficult to cut.

When we visited Emmie Baker in Moor Lane, we used to go down Hawes Lane, passed the tip where we used to fly our kites. A lot of elder bushes grew there and when the elder flowers were out we used to collect some. Granny used to make an infusion of elder flower tea. It was quite pleasant to drink. Some people used to collect a lot and they made elder flower wine, and later, when the berries were ripe they made elderberry wine. We never made any. Mom never brewed beer either because we didn't drink any. Lots of other people did however. Home brewed ale was very popular.

Haden Hill Park became a popular place to visit. I remember long avenues of rhododendrons, always called 'Whitsuntide Bosses' by Grandad Hodgetts, making big splashes of colour, pink, cerise, and white, all the way down to the lake. I don't think I realized at all that the whole of this had been a private garden. Our garden was a patch of soil about six foot by four, just a hearthrug size really. In the spring there were bluebells in the woods at the park. We were used to seeing bluebells growing in the hedgerows and up the banks, but I couldn't believe my eyes when I saw them growing like a deep blue carpet at Haden Hill. Many times later I was to see other places with even more bluebells, but they have never had the same impact as the first time I saw them at Old Hill. Some-times we went there for a picnic. That gave us more time to explore. Mom and sometimes Aunt Mary Jane, would sit together and chat, while Uncle Horace and Dad went for a walk, with May, Doris, and me, and Arthur and Stanley, running around about somewhere around them. It was a favourite place on Sunday nights too, in the summer. They had a brass band playing on the band stand, and there were lots of people sitting about, and walking about. It was a chance to wear one's Sunday best clothes, and really feel good and relaxed. The walking was always at a very leisurely pace, with frequent stops as other families that we knew met us, and we all stopped to chat. It was a very social thing.

As we grew older we were able to go there without our parents. A few sandwiches and a bottle of water, or cold tea, made a grand picnic for us. The sandwiches were most likely to be jam. Home-made black currant, gooseberry, or damson, as a general rule. Mom did make blackberry and apple too, but as we all liked this in pies too it was rare for this to last to the end of the winter, never mind the Spring. If we were very tired when it was time to come home, we used to come back from the Crown, on the tramcar. We used to keep the fare tied up in the corner of our handkerchief so that we did not lose it or be tempted to spend it on sweets. . These trams had long seats along each side. They were made of slatted wood which always seemed to cut my legs. If the weather was hot I used to stick to the varnish. Going up or down a steep incline meant tilting sideways towards the lower end, and swinging round bends tended to overbalance everybody over to the other side of the tram. I always preferred travelling with a grown-up who could keep a tight hold on me. Because Waterfall Lane was too steep for the trams to run up and down a new road was built, Perry Park Road, but it was always known as 'The Tump'.

There was one form of transport which you may not have heard much about, this was known as a 'brake'. I can only recall going on one once myself, although I must have been taken for trips previous to that, a silly thing brings it to mind. One of the current music hall songs popular at that time was called "Horsey, keep your tail up', and everybody seemed to sing it on the way home. I talked to Mr. 'Ted' Siviter about this, it was his father who owned the brake, and he said that as far as he can recall his father stopped using the brake about 1922. Mrs. Minnie Westwood once showed me a photograph of a whole crowd of girls, Mom included, who went on a trip to Bearwood, to visit Warley Abbey, now demolished. The fare for this was sixpence each. (two and half pence new money.)

Trips were run to Clent, the Lickey Hills, Kinver, Bewdley and Stourport, and so on. This seemed to entail a very early start, and, according to some older people I have spoken to, the risk of not getting to your chosen destination. I heard mention of lost wheels, horses going lame, or casting a shoe, which sometimes meant that the next village one came to was 'Hobson's Choice' as far as that trip was concerned. None of the ladies seemed to mind however. The journey was the main thing, and of course, the company. The destination seemed to be of secondary importance.

Later we were to go by charabanc. Venturing as far as Worcester, Stratford-on-Avon, and Tintern Abbey. The seats were in long rows across the body, with seperate doors for each row. The top was open to the elements, but if it did come on to rain, one could put up one's umbrella! The next models had a hood which had to be opened concertina fashion from the back to the front, proving some protection overhead from the downpour, but not at the sides, that came later still, with thick celluloid that always seemed to be a funny yellow shade. I remember also that these vehicles had a very low boiling point, and when we got to steep hill all able bodied persons got out and walked, while the charabanc chugged painfully to the top. There it would wait for the walkers while cooling off the engine.

When we went to Birmingham, we used to go 'by train. From the Village we used to go across Bell End to a point almost opposite Park Avenue, then turn right down station Fields. This was a rough path with hedges on one side and a pit mound on the other. Actually, when this mound was levelled and houses erected, it was always known to us as the Mount Estate. Britannia Road was made, and it became more pleasant to walk to and from the station, but this was not until the late 1920's, up to that time there was just this awful obstacle race of a path with its ruts, mud, stones, and stiles, to be negotiated. I know Mom hated it. She told me how the girls always tried to keep in little groups on their way home from work. Rumours spread fast, either true or false, and they feared men with open razors who would try to cut off a girl's long plaits. There was a good market for long hair, and Mom's hair was thick and beautiful, and long enough to sit on, and being lame she could never run very fast.

Aunt Martha used to take me to the pantomine, and Mom used to take me to get material for our new clothes. But I remember best going to the station with Dad on Sunday nights to get his weekly season ticket ready for Monday morning. This was when he was working at the brickyard at Solihull. They had to take a chimney stack down part way, then rebuild it high, and Solihull was too far to walk every day even for Dad. I used to go out on to the platform to watch for a train, and I was thrilled to bits when one arrived while I was standing there. Years later, when I had to stand on that platform at seven in the morning, in biting wind, and freezing sleet, I could never work up much enthusiasm, unless it was the train I happened to be waiting for. Nestle's chocolate out of the station slot machine still tasted as good however.

The first time I saw the sea I went by train. I was about eight years old, and in common with a lot of other children, I had never been to the sea-side. The L.M.S. Railway advertised an excursion train from Spon Lane station to visit Blackpool. Mom decided to take me, and Aunt Eliza took Dora and Gwen. We got up at three o'clock and Dad walked with us all the way to Spon Lane.

Looking back now, it must have been a terrible journey for Mom, but she never complained. The station platform was crowded, it seemed everyone was taking advantage of this trip. the fare I think was four shillings and sixpence, but when the train came in we all managed to squeeze on, and as soon as the guard blew ,his whistle, waved his flag, and jumped into the van; the porters finished slamming doors, the engine gave a toot, and slowly we steamed out of the station, amidst much shouting and waving, and then we realised that, like Dad, lots of people had not come to catch the train themselves, but had come to help others to the station, and to wave them off. A visit to the sea-side was still a novelty for lots of us you see.

Aunt Polly and Uncle Jack, with Arthur and Jack junior had gone to Blackpool for a fortnight's holiday, and by one of Fate's little ironies, we bumped straight into them when we walked out of the station, heading for the sea-front. We were all amazed. There were more people in Blackpool than I had imagined in the whole of England. They poured out of the station like bees out of a hive, as various excursion trains disgorged their load. Crowds pressed in on every side as we stopped to chat. We were excited, and impatient to see the sand, and the sea, and Arthur and Jack were eager to show us everything that they had seen on their holiday. We were all bubbling over, but Uncle Jack took the lead, and steered us all safely over the widest road that I had ever seen; and then, there was the beach, and the sea. I felt absolutely petrified! I just could not believe it. Pictures which I had seen had given no indication of the vast limitless expanse of water which now lay before us. I just stared in amazement, and when Aunt Polly told us to look behind us, and there was the famous Tower, I felt really bewildered. We had to put our heads right back to see the top. Not that we were on our own. There were cries of delight, and dismay from all around us, as other people saw these things for the first time. I doubt if you, who have seen the sea all your lives, will ever understand the awe which we felt when we saw it that first time.

We went down on to the beach to eat our sandwiches, and to have a cup of tea out of our new thermos flask, then, with shoes and socks off, we went into the sea to have a paddle. It was colder than I had expected, but we didn't stay in very long. There was too much to see, and to do, and not very much time to do it in. The tide was going out, and as the beach widened, the crowds were flocking on to the sand. From a distance it looked as though a fly couldn't get through, but it wasn't so bad really when you were down there yourself.

A stroll along the sea front sounded like a cross between Rowley Wake and the Birmingham Bull Ring on a Saturday Night. In the jostle of the crowd I don't remember very much. Eye level to a child in a crowd is usually the below waist view of the people in front. Later we took a tramcar to the boarding-house where Arthur and Jack were staying. Everybody brought their own food in these places, and with the landlady's permission, we were able to go in and Aunt Polly prepared our tea. Afterwards we made a leisurely way back to the station to get the excursion train back home.

After such an exciting day, the journey home was a bit of an anti-climax, and having been up since three, we were glad to sleep on the way back. Dad was waiting for us at Spon Lane, and we had the long walk back home before climbing sleepily into bed, in my case, taking a little package with me. As we had passed the Tower on our way to the station, Uncle Jack bought me a little purse on a chain. It was made of a kind of waxed, red cloth, and the outside was covered with mother of pearl shell, painted on the front with a small spray of flowers, and 'A Present from Blackpool' written on it. It cost one shilling and threepence, and I thought it was beautiful, and I loved it on sight. The shell was so smooth to the touch, and it changed to all the colours of the rainbow as you moved it about in the light. I used it until the cloth rotted and slit. Then I wrapped it in tissue paper and put it in a drawer. Years and years later, I unwrapped my little parcel and I was very sad when I found the shell crumbled to bits, and my 'Present from Blackpool' had to be thrown away but thankfully, memory remains.

It was another two years before I went to the sea side again. By now the excursion day trips had become very popular, and from school we had visited London Zoo, Rhyl, Weston-super-Mare, and Blackpool. As trade picked up in some quarters, so more people began to go to the sea for a holiday. Not that holidays were new. Some people had always been able to go on holiday, but they had gone to places near to their homes, and, for the Midlands, anywhere near to the coast was the farthest distance to go, so mostly, the sea-side was excluded. Aunt Martha and Emmie Baker used to go on holiday together. Like Aunt Polly at Blackpool, they stayed in boarding houses. Twice I went with them to Rhyl. We paid one pound each to Mason's Coaches for the fare, and one pound each to the landlady at the boarding house. This paid for one's bed, and the cooking done by the landlady. We provided our own food. Every day after breakfast, we went shopping. We each put a pound in the kitty, and Emmie usually managed on that. Helping her mother at home with the family, she was used to handling housekeeping money, and doing the catering. It was no use living well at the beginning of the week and then have nothing left for the last few days. Meat and vegetables were handed in before eleven, and when we went back for our dinner they were brought out from the kitchen in labelled vegetable dishes. This type of accommodation dropped out later in favour of small hotels, but after the war, when maids were more difficult to obtain, lots of these hotels were converted into self-contained flats.

The fare for the coach is interesting. The charabanc had given way to the coach. Not the air-conditioned luxury we enjoy to-day, but a distinct improvement nevertheless. The coach proprietors had shown great shrewdness. For a short period during the summer they ran a weekly coach to the more popular resorts, taking holiday makers one week, and bringing them back the next, as they still do. They scored over the railways by being able to guarantee a seat, with no bother over luggage, or changing trains. No pushing, crowding, or waiting for a train which might well be full before it pulled into the station. Crewe station was notorious for this changing about. As it was, we took our luggage to Masons on the Friday night, and when we went to Oldbury Road on

Saturday morning, it was already stowed away in the back. We left Blackheath about seven, and arrived at Rhyl before dinner without any fuss or bother.

We still used the trains quite a lot however. To and from work every day; and excursions were still popular too. If you were a small party it was possible to reserve a carriage or two, if you were a larger party, then you could reserve a coach. I remember going to Rhyl with the Social circle from Chapel this way. On the return journey we were pulled on to a siding for two hours, and we none of us realised it. Mr. John Dallow was telling us Black Country stories, of which he had an unlimited repertoire, some of which were true, and we were so busy laughing that time just slipped by.

If you could organise a trainload, then it was quite easy to book a train. This method was very popular with firms who took their employees for an annual outing.

You may well be asking by now where all those dreams of faraway places went to. Well I'm afraid that is all they ever were, just dreams. One minor miracle happened in 1970. I went with Lesley to Oberammergau to see the Passion Play. We went through Switzerland, Austria, Germany, and Leichtenstein. It was a marvellous experience which still seems to have an air of unreality about it. Some things I will always remember. The Olympic ski-run at Innsbruck, the Alps, and a fabulous journey through the Brenner Pass, where in a few short hours we passed from the deep snow of Winter at the top, slowly descending through the days of Springtime, until the last of the hairpin bends brought us to the full bloom of roses in early Summertime, at the bottom.

We went to Amsterdam, for the day, but as for all the rest of the travelling, I have practically given up thinking about it. Years ago I began to hear tales of scorpions in beds, and snakes in shoes, armies of ants on the rampage, and all kinds of stinging insects, and I am one who can get hysterics if I find a big spider in the bath, so I came to the conclusion that if I had to go to these places I should have to get myself enclosed in a glass case, so that I could see out, but nothing could get at me. Well, some clever gentleman has done better than that. Instead of me having to wear a cumbersome suit, he has left me free to go about my own business here, and he enclosed everything else in a glass case so that I come to no harm. He called it Television. Now I can climb any mountain, cross any desert, or snowy waste, search for lost tribes with David Attenborough, or study botany with David Bellamy. I am the perfect Armchair Traveller; and it is far cheaper too.

INTO THE TWENTIES

At some time after Uncle Wilf had been de-mobbed, Uncle Horace, Dad, and Uncle Wilf joined forces. Dad no longer worked at British Cyanides, and I suppose he was eager to get back to his own trade. They took on a project at a brick yard at Solihull to lower a chimney stack, and then to re-build it higher. This must have been about 1923. I remember it because one Saturday morning Dad took me with him on the train to the site. When we came away at lunch time I was proudly bearing some half-dozen bulrushes which someone had fetched for me from the marl-hole. I could not remember ever seeing any before.

When we arrived home, Mom put them in a big vase and placed them on a palm stand in the corner. At a later date we came downstairs one morning to find the room full of bulrush seeds. Millions of them. They were floating in the air like an airborne army. Each little seed carried on its own parachute, waiting to land. No such things then as a vacuum cleaner, everything had to be taken outside on to the backyard and brushed. They were worse than feathers.

The sealed tomb of King Tut-ankh-Amen was opened in Luxor at this time. I didn't know anything about it then but I enjoyed seeing the artifacts when they were exhibited in London a few years ago. Lesley and I waited for four hours one very hot day to get into the British Museum, and I would willingly do it all over again for the chance of a second look.

The Duke of York married Lady Elizabeth Bowes-Lyon on the twenty-sixth of April, and nobody dreamed that one day they would become our much loved King and Queen because everybody had such high hopes of the Price of Wales being a perfect King.

Two days after the Royal Wedding, the first Association Football Cup Final was played at Wembley. The crowds were so enormous that they broke down the barriers.

I was five years old now and able to go to school, officially. You have heard of children playing truant from school, well I played truant from home to sneak off to school at every opportunity. It took me a long time to master the gate at school, but sometimes someone had not fastened it properly and I was able to get in. I soon found out which was the babies class and joined in with the rest of the children.

Crossword puzzles, which I enjoy, first appeared this year, but I was too young to know or care then, or that the chimes of 'Big Ben' were first broadcast. We did not have a 'cat's whisker' radio set, the so-called wireless, so we did not listen to '2 LO Calling'. Reading, and being read to were my favourite pastimes, also cutting Magyars (dresses and blouses cut out without a set-in sleeve) from paper, and lining them up on strings to sell in a shop, or to dress my dolls. I had one china doll with black hair cut in a' bob' and with a fringe. These were known as 'Joan' dolls, and the hair cut was very fashionable. I had mine cut like it for years. I think they were named after Joan Crawford, the film star. I know that when I was very young I had a doll on a stick. It had three legs on a sort of wheel, and as you pushed it along it looked like someone walking. This too was named after a Film star. Mary Pickford, star of the silent film days.

It was about this time that I went to the first wedding that I can remember. Aunt Eliza's eldest daughter, Lily, was married to Arthur Rollason. It was a white wedding, with the bridesmaids in blue with silver lace panels on the side skirt. She was I believe the first bride in the Village to go to church by motor car. I had a ride in this car, from the church back to Granny Hodgetts' house. It was my first ride in a car and I hated it. I couldn't see a thing and I felt I never wanted to go in a dickey seat again, nor did I.

When I was seven I moved from the Infants School at Currall Road, but instead of going to 'the big school' at Siviter's Lane, I was sent to The Church of England School at Hawes Lane. Uncle Joe Chater gave me a Prayer Book bound in green Morocco leather, and a Hymns Ancient and Modern, in Blue. The Headmaster was Mr. Hopcroft, he lived in the house which is now the Rowley Conservative Club, and the school came under the jurisdiction of the Vicar, at that time Rev. Cheverton.

I soon settled down to the routine of the new school. I had, fortunately, a retentive memory, and soon learned the collects, and enjoyed the novelty of visits to Church on special Holy Days, and the Armistice Day Service. I have no doubt we were informed of any important news items of the day, like Amunsden and Ellsworth flying the dirigible Norge, Spitzbergen - North Pole - Alaska; and the American R.E.Byrd making a first aeroplane flight to the North Pole, and our own Alan Cobham flew to Capetown and back in the Spring, and managed to fly to Melbourne and back in the early Autumn. Then there was the National strike. It only lasted a fortnight but it caused a great upheaval.

I am quite sure there was a lot of discussion also about the League of Nations. So much was hoped for it. War would be no more and all that. It didn't work. There was, and still is, wars, and rumours of wars.

Local changes began taking place however that did affect the family very much. Council houses were built at Blackheath, and Aunt Eliza, Uncle Joe, Bill, Bert, Dora and Gwen, were moved from Granny's house to Central Avenue. Mr. Aldridge who owned the house now needed it for one of his daughters, so when Mr. and Mrs Parsons and Irene moved to Belbroughton with Mr. Tom Williams, Mom arranged a transfer from our house to the one next door and Granny, Grandad and Aunt Martha, came to live with us.

There was nothing out of the ordinary about this. When people became old or ill, and could no longer work, the family needed to rally round. If it was a large family I have known it being made possible for parents to stay in their own home by each member making a small contribution each week. Sometimes the old home was broken up and the older folk went to live with one of their children. When the Old Age pension Act came into force it paid seven shillings and sixpence for a couple, or five shillings for a single person, but they had to be over seventy. This was probably a big help to some, although if the average rent was half a crown a week it wouldn't leave much to live on. If all else failed of course they had to go to the workhouse.

Many bitter tears were shed when this happened. I vividly remember one old man in particular, sobbing and pleading with his daughter and son-in-law, as he tottered a few steps behind them up the hill. Crying "Do' send me to the workhus our wench, let me stop at wum, I wo ate much."

Granny and Grandad had the back bedroom, Aunt Martha shared my room which was over the front parlour, and Mom and Dad had the front bedroom over the living room. In this living room we had a large dining table, an assortment of dining chairs, Granny's large chest of drawers, a sofa, a Windsor armchair. a large fitment in the recess between the fireplace and window which had belonged to the shop, and several podged rugs on the quarry floor, also on the wall opposite the fireplace we had an American Organ and Mom's Singer sewing machine. In the parlour we had a seven piece suite covered in plum coloured rexine. One couch, one Gentleman's Armchair, one Ladies Armchair, and four dining chairs. One wall was completely taken up with our big sideboard. There was no fireplace in this room.

It was quite a roomy house. Between our living room and the large back kitchen was a smaller living room with a half-range grate and Granny and Grandad decided to live in that, but Grandad came in to us quite often to have a game of dominoes or draughts, in the evenings. One thing I never liked about this house was the toilet. It was outside, and across the yard. It was to be 1953 before I had the luxury of an indoor toilet again.

Most of our enjoyment was home-made. We did not go to the pictures although it was fashionable to do so. We went to see 'Ben Hur' with Ramon Navarro at the King's Theatre, Blackheath, because that was a religious film, but we did not go to see Al Jolson in the 'Jazz Singer' although everyone was talking about it. From school we were taken to the Pavilion, High Street, Blackheath, to see 'Uncle Tom's Cabin', and we were also taken there to see the 'Life of David Livingstone'.

Amelia Earhart became the first woman to fly the Atlantic, and Britain won the Schneider Trophy for sea planes, at a speed of 281 m.p.h., but planes were still a novelty to us. We used to stand still and watch until it went out of sight. Cars were becoming more frequent now. Dr. Beasley had the first one in Rowley. and the Midland Red began a bus service to Dudley. They used to deliver the papers too, as they came by Tibbetts's shop the bus conductor used to throw them out to the waiting paper boys.

From school we went on a train to London Zoo. We used to go to Birmingham on the train, but I think this was the first long journey that I made. To be on a train with a corridor, this was really travelling. I felt as excited as if I had been on the 'Orient Express'.

We did not go far from home at this time. Granny could not now get upstairs by herself and every night when she was ready to go to bed Dad took her up the stairs. He would walk home no matter where we were. Get her upstairs to bed, and then come back for us. At last she had to stay in bed. I did not realize how ill she was until Granny Hadley and the aunts began to sit up with her. I was just eleven years old when she died in 1929. Dora, Gwen, and I each had a navy blue Melton -cloth coat. This I think was the first time that I had a ready to wear coat.

Elsie Clifford in Hawes Lane was a Tailoress and she always made our dresses, coats, and costumes, and especially my Anniversary dresses. But as we had to have them in a hurry I think Aunt Nance got all of them from the Warehouse in Birmingham.

The undertakers had some fine black horses at this time. They used to look lovely at funerals resplendent with black ribbons and tall black ostrich feathers. The hearse too would be be-decked likewise. However, as we lived so near to the Church, George Beese, the Verger and Gravedigger, brought the bier to the door and the coffin was placed upon it. The bearers and mourners following on foot across Church Road to the entrance to the Churchyard.

It was the custom then for people to line the pavement with bowed heads, and all the men took off their hats. If any work was being done in the street the workmen too stopped and waited silently until after the cortege had passed, and all the neighbours would draw their curtains.

I was very pre-occupied about this time about school. A new housing estate had been completed, and in Britannia Road a new school was being built. We had heard lots of discussions on schools in general and we had heard that Siviter's Lane was not to be a mixed school anymore but a Senior Girls School, and the new Britannia Road School was for Senior Boys. But we belonged to the Church and I did not think at first that we were affected. I was very comfortable where I was, thank you very much, and I did not wish to change. I had passed the examination for Wright's Lane Secondary School the year before as a test before taking the equivalent of the 'Eleven Plus', and had been bitterly disappointed when Dad said 'No' to any homework. After the initial shock I had settled down again and we were all very surprised when we were told that we were being closed down and that after the hop-picking holiday we should be going to our respective new schools.

So September that year proved to be a very apprehensive month. I missed Gran. Grandad was upset and cried for his 'old lady' as he called her. Aunt Polly had given birth to Howard in the June and the chat always seemed to be babies this, that, and the other. I didn't realise until later that it was because Mom was expecting a baby herself, although I still did not know when. We were not so precocious in those days, and I wondered also what was to become of me. I think I was expecting to be sent away when Mom had a baby of their own. Hilda arrived safely on Boxing Day 1929, and I stayed put. They never realised how worried I had been.

The Housing Act to clear slum property was going well. The Council had inspected nearly all the cottages in the Village and condemned them. New houses were being built between Church Road and Mincing Lane. It was called New Hall Road, Rowley Hall being across Church Road, but we still called it across the 'Quack'. Aunt Emily and Uncle Jack had moved to Limes Avenue, Aunt Beck and Uncle Bill to the new houses at the lower end of the Village, but nearly all the others were moved one after the other, into New Hall Road. It was like playing draughts. When Aunt Beck moved out, Aunt Martha asked if she could move in. Albert Taylor owned the property and he let her have the key.

Poor Grandad. He didn't want to go. The night Granny died he had asked that he might die where his 'old lady' had died and Dad had promised that as far as he was concerned, so he should, but now he had to go.

Granny Hadley also had to move. Uncle Wilf had married Aunt Lil. Eventually they went to live in a council house in Oldbury Road. Granny went to live with Aunt Polly. It is sad to see a home broken up. Queen Victoria was lifted down from the fireplace wall. I never saw the picture again, nor did I ever hear Granny Hadley speak of her any more.

We had had new neighbours too. First we had had Mr. and Mrs. Lane and Mary. Funny the little things which stay in the mind. I always remember that Mrs. Lane always used 'Lux' soap for washing Mary, and the day the Prince of Wales opened the New Wolverhampton Road he went to Lench's Park. Mrs. Lane shook hands with him there and when she came home she laughingly declared that she was never going to wash that hand again. I thought it very odd. After they went to live at Blackheath Mr. and Mrs Hewitt and family came to live there.

ROWLEY WAKE

Rowley Wake always took place during the early days of September. Traditionally a time for engaging labour, and for the buying and selling of horses and other livestock. Rowley Church is dedicated to St Giles, the patron saint of cripples, and the saint's day is September the First so , I think it is safe to say that the fair was tied up at one time to the saint's Holy Day. Nearly every village had a similar Fair, or Wake, now only the pleasure side seems to remain, and even that is dwindling. Then it was a once a year occurrence, now fairgrounds are permanent fixtures at pleasure grounds in all resorts. At one time our Fair seemed to get bigger and bigger, and the equipment more sophisticated, but nowadays they are nothing to write home about, one reason for this is I suppose the lack of fairgrounds. Most of the old traditional sites have been used for building purposes.

I can remember it being on ground by the George and Dragon in Blackheath High Street, down Oldbury Road, near to the site occupied by the Regis Heath estate, and at Whiteheath on the corner of Oldbury Road and Throne Road. But the site I remember best is the one at Hurst Green. The entrance to the fairground was just about where Kinith's Way is now. The field was always known as Fairfield. I wonder if that is why Fairfield Road was so called. There is also a Fairfield public house.

When we were older, towards eleven or twelve maybe, we used to go to Hurst Green to watch the arrival of the caravans and lorries, and to raise a cheer when we saw the first vehicle marked "Pat Collins'. It never seemed possible that all those gaily painted roundabouts could be packed up into such a small space. We always stayed until the last possible minute, heedless of the meal waiting for us at home. Hating to miss each new arrival receiving his orders about parking his living van, and where he was to erect his particular part of the fair.

We walked home buoyed up with anticipation. Knowing that the next time we saw the fairground it would be transformed. A veritable wonderland. The drab everyday ordinary surroundings would be completely forgotten, eyes blinded to them by the other senses focusing totally upon the madly whirling roundabouts, the brilliant lights, and the raucous shouting of the barkers mingling with the music of the splendid organs, and the hub-hub of the jostling crowds. Then there was the smell of the gingerbread and the brandy snaps, the roast potatoes and hot chestnuts, and the special smell of hot oil from the steam engines.

Being on holiday from school for the month, we went to the fair on the Monday afternoon with our mothers. Then it was possible to have a ride on the roundabouts, and go in the sideshows, in comparative comfort. But to see the fair at its best, one had to go at night, Some of course went every night, Friday to Tuesday, which was Carnival Night; but we never did. Dad used to take me on Saturdays, just after tea. It used to seem as though everybody on earth was going to the fair. The roads were thronged with people. It would have been impossible to miss the way there. Looking down from the top of the hill we could see a big bright glow, and everyone was heading for the centre of it, drawn irresistibly forward like iron filings towards a magnet, footsteps getting faster as the noise began to reach the ears, impelling feet to move more quickly, until we were completely engulfed by the light, the heat, the smell, the incredible noise, and the close-packed throng.

The safest place to be then, was up in the air, and when I was small, Dad used to lift me up and hoist me on to his shoulders. I liked it up there; the whole fairground lay like a panorama before me. The “Golden Gallopers” whirling around, going up and down, up and down, but never getting anywhere, the beautifully polished, barley-sugar twisted brass poles, gleaming in the bright lights. ‘The Dragons” roaring round faster and faster, rising and falling on the undulating floor, the girls screaming and laughing, gripping the handrail tightly. Even the organ seemed to be playing faster. The “Chair-o-Planes’ scared me to death. To see the chairs swinging out further and further as they rose higher and higher to the level of the stand, always made me feel sick, and I broke out in a cold sweat. The “Steam Boats” too I never liked. They were huge cage-like contraptions, usually two, swinging in opposite directions; they would swing higher and higher until they were almost upside down, and squeals of delighted fear from the passengers and onlookers alike, used to mingle with the music of the organs, and the spiel of the barkers, making that curious cacophony of sound which to me at any rate is synonymous with fairgrounds.

As the crowd milled about, surging forward, or back, as people tried to leave the rides, or get on to them, it was impossible to choose any particular direction in which to move. Usually they were a good-natured bustling throng, and eventually one would come to a place where the crowds were a little thinner, and change direction then, Interspersed amongst the roundabouts were the other amusements, like the “Cake Walk”, the “Dodgem Cars”, and the “Whip”; the tall wooden “Helter Skelter”, the crowds shouting with glee when someone came adrift from their mat, and had a hot seat in consequence. Then there was “Roll-a-Penny”, and “Fruit Machines”. They are called “One-Arm Bandits” nowadays, and they never seem to pay out a jackpot like they used to do. Then they needed a hat or cap to catch all the pennies as they cascaded out, to the whoops of delight from the winner and watchers alike.

The “Swing Boats” with their big fluffy ‘sallies’ always seemed to do good business, and so did the children’s swings and roundabouts. On these, the man himself wielded a mangle-like contraption, and could control the speed of the roundabout, turning faster or slower, according to the type of children that he was carrying. There was also the kind of stalls where one bought a ticket, like a lottery game; there were several variations, like the names of Railway stations, or Cities, Famous Racehorses, or Greyhounds, sometimes even Film Stars. Whatever names were used, the winner was declared after the light had stopped on a section, and if your ticket had the same name on it, then you won the prize. For years I wanted a big coloured ball, but we never won one.

Circling the perimeter of the field were the sideshows and booths. Coconuts

Shies, and Aunt Sallies, Rifle Shooting, Dart Throwing, Ball Rolling, and the Fortune Teller. Dad would carefully make a tour of these. Stopping *in* front of each one in turn so that we could see what was going on. Standing longer in front of the booths where the performers were doing a small part of their act, to whet the appetite of the watchers, and lure them into the tent. The Fire-Eater with his flaming torch, the Strong Man bending iron bars. The Tattooed Man, sometimes the Tattooed Lady too, exposing one arm from under a gaudy cloak, with an invitation to step inside and see some more, after paying your money of course.

The first coloured man I ever remember seeing was at the fair. He was in the Boxing booth. Then there was the usual collection of Oddities, The Fat Lady, and the Bearded Lady, Dwarfs and Manikins. The Illusionist with his mesmerising tricks. How do they get those girl's heads balancing on spider's webs? You know you are being fooled, but can never understand how. Jugglers, Stiltmen, and so-called wild Animals, there is room for them all at the fair.

Speaking of animal acts, I remember Dad telling me that years ago there was one called Casher's, or Casha's Dancing Ducks. Someone reported this to the police, and when they had inspected the act, they prosecuted him. The poor ducks danced alright, he was putting them on hot bricks. The Scoundrel.

A visit to see the wonderful steam traction engines was always a must. The heat, the noise, the smell, the man with his inevitable oil can and oily rag. It was a fascinating sight, but then, with head spinning, one left the ground with a mixture of relief and regret. As soon as we were clear of the ground, dusty or muddy, depending upon the weather, we would set off for home, leaving hardier souls behind, they would probably be there until midnight.

The walk back home, up Rowley Hill took longer to trudge than the walk down had done. No bright glow to lead the way, and the stirring music grew fainter to our ears as we walked past the people still hurrying down.

After reaching home I was allowed one curl of Brandy Snap, and meanwhile Dad would carefully open the Coconut, which was won if you were lucky, and bought, if one was not. He used to cut the eyes open at the top of the nut and strain the milk into a cup and I drank it with relish. It was food for the gods. Champagne and Caviar? They could never taste so good.

Looking up Rowley Village

And down

BONFIRE NIGHT.

Much preparation went into the making of a good bonfire. Very few people had their own garden, or yard. Most were shared yards with six or more houses all using it for drying washing - so individual bonfires were out, and sometimes the people who shared the yard, shared the bonfire. In some cases two or three yards would join together and pool their resources to make one big bonfire, - known colloquially as a 'boster'.

Young and old alike worked with a will. During the long school holiday in September, spare time would be spent in collecting 'bats' from the old coal tips. Nearly all the families with children had an old dobbin for trundling heavy goods about. This was usually an old wooden soap box, they were wood then, not cardboard fibre like they are today, begged from the local grocer, and mounted on two wheels, generally from an old pram, or bassinette, and two pieces of wood fastened firmly to the sides for handles. These would be chamfered off at the ends for a better grip. If you were very lucky and managed to get the handles from the bassinette, so much the better, because then, when you were going up hill you could step inside the handles, and, being like a pony drawing a trap, had more pulling power.

Quite a large portion of the old tips must have been moved in this manner, and stored away in the corners of the yards, or the nail shops, often accompanied by the irate voice of some busy housewife whose washing would be hanging on the line. Every day was wash day on a shared yard because every house had its own day in turn, and when you took over the tenancy, you took over that day to do your washing. So if the weather was bad, or you were ill, or in this case, if dirty little scamps, of both sexes, got covered in coal dust, and brushed passed the wet washing and it had to be rinsed again, then there was the possibility that it wouldn't dry that day so it often meant an angry exchange of words; but the bat collecting still went on.

Fireworks were purchased with money coaxed from friends or relations, for doing odd jobs, or running errands. Some of the older boys and men used to make their own. Long Jack-the-Rappers with as many as twenty-four folds. Enough to make everybody jump out of the way. Then of course there was always the old Penny for the Guy routine, with the Guy being paraded about in the aforementioned conveyance, the dobbin. Naturally, there was always rivalry amongst the community as to who had the best Guy. Speaking personally I think they were works of art. Nothing like the shapeless bundles thrown on to the fires today, and called a Guy. Ours were practically life-sized.

Aunt Emily's George and Fred Horton made the best I ever saw. Two suitable lengths of wood were lashed together to form a cross. An old boiler suit, or even a large pair of combinations was put over this for a body, and the whole thing was stuffed well. Wood Shavings, sawdust, old paper and rags, anything that came to hand. An old pair of shoes was attached to the bottom for feet, the sole eased slightly away from the uppers so that five slim fireworks were inserted for toes. A pair of gloves, also stuffed, was used for the hands, woolen ones were best for this, then the fireworks could be threaded through the stitches. The jacket was put on, and where the buttons should be, small Catherine Wheels were nailed through to the wood underneath. Wood shavings, all curly made hair, a mask for a face, pretty paper or rag made a muffler, and a hat of sorts, depending upon whatever anyone was throwing away that year, one year it was a silk top hat, but always, fireworks around the crown, and a rocket down the back of the neck. They were beautiful.

Everybody who could took a hand in the preparation. The bats were sorted out and the large ones made into a ring on the ground. It was rather like building an igloo really. When you got about a couple of feet up a row of tins were built in. These were usually Libby's Corned Beef tins, seven pound size. They would have been carefully collected over the weeks, scalded, dried, and put safely away ready for the bonfire. These were used as ovens, baked potatoes and chestnuts were very popular. After the last row of big bats had been places in position, the centre would be filled in with the remaining bats, and all the accumulated rubbish which had been collected. Some paper, wood and coal were used to get it stated, if it was damp weather it sometimes needed a shovelful or two of fire carried out of the grate, but once it got going the heat was terrific.

An assortment of seats were placed round the fire, after you had made sure which way the wind was blowing, if you didn't want to be choked with smoke that is. Stools, backless chairs, turned-up boxes, or planks laid upon piles of bricks, anything was utilised. Much as today, the sky began to take on a red glow just after tea, and the air was filled with smoke and the acrid taste of gunpowder. People began trafficking about looking in at one fire or another, or going to the various public houses, each of whom had their own bonfire, and a free issue of 'Grorty Pudding'. I wonder if they salted it well!

We also had 'Grorty Pudding'. All day it had been cooking in the biggest stewjar, in the back of the oven. Groats, onions, meat. I can't say which was the most delicious, the smell wafting out of the oven, making everyone pick up their noses and sniff, or the delicious taste of it as one sat by the fire, with hot baked potatoes, on the side, all fluffy, and enough butter to overflow and run down the chin.

At last came the burning of the 'Guy'. The sparklers and the fireworks had been let off, and then we were ready for the last act. I don't know how other people managed, but at Aunt Emily's we had a chain slung over the top of the bonfire using the washing line hooks usually used by Aunt Emily and Mrs. Toye, and the 'Guy' was hauled along on a sort of pulley system until he dangled over the centre of the fire. Almost immediately his toes would catch fire and the scene around the bonfire would glow with the intense light and colour of the different fireworks. The old shoes would drop to the fire and the legs would quickly burn. Then the Catherine Wheels would begin to whirr and sparkle, flames would run along the arms, and his fingers would glow. Muffler, face, hair, hat, each in turn would ignite the other, the flames eventually reaching out to the touchpaper on the rocket. with a loud whoosh! and a shower of sparks it would soar up into the air along with our whoops of delight. The wooden framework of the 'Guy', now burning fiercely, was safely lowered on to the bonfire to finish burning away, and one by one, everybody made their way home. Tired stinking of smoke, but happy.

Around the corner, in Church Road, stood Rowley Hall, just over three hundred years before, in 1605, Humphrey Lyttleton and Robert Winter, fleeing from capture following the arrest of Guy Fawkes in London, eventually made their way there and were sheltered in the cellars, by the owner Christopher White. He was related to the Lyttletons of Holbeache House at Kingswinford, who was also involved in the trouble.

Later on, two men, Thomas Holyhead, and another, not apparently Mr. White, were hanged for sheltering the fugitives. We had the original history on our doorsteps, and we never even gave it a thought.

Mincing Lane

EDUCATION

Education will I suppose, always be a vexed question. Some like to go to school, and some hate it. Some want to stay as long as they can, and get to university or college. Some regard any learning at all to be a complete waste of time, and they are quite prepared to fritter their lives away, and unfortunately, everybody else's time, waiting for the day when they can get out. Even now, with all the modern equipment available, students are playing truant for the silliest of reasons. I am happy to say that even though our schools were poorly equipped in comparison with most modern schools, I loved to go, and I was full of regret when I had to leave.

I began school at Currall Road Infants just before I was five. Miss. Caddick, the headmistress, let me start as soon as she could because I haunted the place at every available opportunity. Mom was always having to fetch me home. This bit of history was to repeat itself later on with Martyn trying to get to Lesley in school, and me having to fetch him home.

We learned the alphabet by chanting it altogether. In fact we learned lots of things by chanting them in unison. To learn to print we had a slate and a slate pencil, and after we had mastered pothooks, we advanced to paper and lead pencil. Proper writing then was copperplate writing so the special paper that we used was marked with feint red lines with two blue lines in between. Our lower case letters fitted in between these blue lines and looped letters above or below had to reach these red lines precisely. Writing was very particular in those days.

Counting was taught by the use of an Abacus, quite a big one, but lots of us had one of these at home, but we just called them counting beads. On the wall we had a large sheet marked off into squares, each square was marked with big pink dots, or little pink balls, whichever way you wanted to look at it, representing the appropriate numbers, rather like the numbers on dominoes. After all these years, if I am tired, or have any difficulty in adding up, I still picture that sheet upon the wall and count up the pink spots.

Action songs were very popular, like Dashing away with the Smoothing Iron, and This is the way we Wash our Hands, this was very popular indeed. When it came to This is the way we stamp our feet, the boys in particular did this with great gusto. The majority of children wore strong boots, not shoes, and these had steel toe and heel tips, so the clatter was enormous. In the playground we played games using bean bags, so much more sensible than balls. They were bigger and more easily caught by clumsy little fingers, and if they were dropped, they stayed put instead of rolling away and wasting time fetching it back. Parts of our playground had a steep slope and dropped balls soon ran down towards the 'big school' and Siviter's Lane.

We danced here to Looby Loo, and In and Out those Darkie Bluebells, and we learned to dodge the farmers when we played Robbers in the Corn. For exercise we played Great Big Giants and Tiny Little Men, doing the appropriate actions, and we ran like mad, screaming with delight when the Wolf shouted 'Dinnertime' when we were playing 'What time is it Mr. Wolf? The sound of children at play is a wonderful thing. Regardless of race or creed, one of the sweetest sounds on earth is the happy laughter of innocent childhood.

In the classroom we were taught the days of the week as per the Nursery Rhyme Soloman Grundy, and another one called the Seven Days, which went like this:

The first day God created light,
And made the day and made the night.
The second day of His intent
He made the heavenly firmament.
The third day came both land and sea,
And grass and herbs, and bush and tree.
The fourth day sun and moon had birth,
And stars that twinkle over earth.
The fifth day, from the waves of strife
God called great creatures into life,
And in the sixth day of His plan,
In his own image God made man.
Then when His work the Lord had blest,
The seventh day He gave to rest.

We learned the rhyme for the months of the year, Thirty Days Hath September, and we had a big calendar on the wall to prove it. The teacher had drawn the illustrations for this with little couplets for each month, beginning 'January brings the snow, makes our feet and fingers glow'. Actually it gave me chilblains, but that wasn't in the rhyme.

The teacher read stories to us, and we heard of the meeting of Little Red Riding Hood and the Wicked Wolf, and scared ourselves with the Giant in Jack and the Beanstalk, but we like to walk around the playground growling Fee Fie Foe Fum, I smell the blood of an Englishman. Be he alive or be he dead, I'll grind his bones to make my bread. We liked Cinderella, and were grieved when she couldn't go to the ball, and cheered when she did, and we all wished that we too could have a Fairy Godmother. In fact I'm still wishing.

We could recite quite a lot of the Mother Goose Nursery Rhymes, and some of the 'Times Tables'. I understand that this learning by chant is frowned upon today. I don't know why. Children love repetition. It is a comfort to them and the memory of things learned this way lasts a lifetime.

Plasticene was provided for handicraft sessions. Which I didn't like, because I couldn't model anything worthwhile, and coloured shiny paper for folding and cutting, and making little lanterns or baskets, or learning to weave, using thin strips, which I did like because I could do that. We learned to knit, using rather thick needles and yarn, and with great pride we took home a kettle holder. We were shown how to tie shoe laces by using cardboard with holes punched in, and a shoe lace. We also learned to sew, using just ordinary running stitch, and how to finish off. We felt very pleased with ourselves when we were able to dress a little celluloid doll. And also we did Cross stitch on canvas, as a start to learning how to do embroidery.

The 'star' system for good work in class was not operating then, but we were given 'cards' for this, and Friday afternoon at close of school, and especially at Christmastime too. This was usually advertising matter, but very interesting all the same. We had paper guns, which went 'Bang', and Whizzers which were discs of thin card on string and they made this whizzing noise as the string was pulled taut and then released again; but, for little girls I suppose the best loved was the Lyons Cap and Apron. The Lyons' Nippy' waitress was very well known then at all the famous Joe Lyons Restaurants, and we all liked to put on our paper replicas and pretend.

When I was seven I was moved to the Church of England School in Hawes Lane. It didn't bother me at all, perhaps because I knew that Dad had attended the same school. It was quite old of course, with no separate classrooms. There was a sliding partition down the centre, and two green cloth curtains sub-divided the halves, but these can hardly be classed as sound-proof. In theory at any rate, we were always supposed to be considerate of the class next door and work as quietly as possible. There was no chanting in unison here, we should have drowned out the voice of the teacher in the next classroom.

In addition to our normal class work we had to learn all the special prayers and collects for the day. I found it a cosy little school. Being small you soon knew everyone who was there, and who was whose sister or brother, or cousin; how old each person was, and what standard they were in.

As at any other school, the lessons began to get more difficult now that we were older. We had to learn to think more quickly, and there was no time for fooling about. I suppose I was lucky, I didn't seem to have much trouble with the lessons, not with the three 'R's' any way. Drawing and modelling, I could not, and still cannot, do. Writing was legible, arithmetic, quite good, reading, first class. I think I must have read more books than all the rest of the class put together. Nursery Rhymes were way behind us now, simple poetry was introduced to us like 'I once Had a Sweet Little Doll Dears', but gradually the pieces got longer and longer, and more complex. The same with reading. We 'did Aesop's Fables, and went on to Lamb's Tales from Shakespeare. We knew that we would eventually graduate to doing the actual plays because we heard the older pupils learning the lines, and Mr. Hopcroft, the Headmaster, taking them through the parts.

History and geography were added to our subjects, and in addition to the simple embroidery, the girls learned to hem. It was not at all exciting. They were blue and white checked material dusters. It needed to be pretty strong to withstand all the unpicking and re-sewing when we could not get our stitches small enough.

We also learned how to do raffia work. We soaked the raffia in water until it was soft and pliable, then we smoothed it out with our fingers to get out all the ridges and creases. Then we made little mats; oblong ones at first, and then round ones. To make a mat we had a piece of strong cardboard a little larger than the size of the mat you wished to make. Along the two short ends of the oblong, and all around the round one, was a serrated edge; then with some thin string you went up and down the card, hooking the string around the serrations. When this was done you wove the raffia in and out of the string, just as we had learned to weave with the thin strips of paper. Not too loose, or the mat was floppy, and not too tight, or the strings gradually tightened and came inwards and that meant you would end up with a 'waisted' mat. Some- times we made them with natural raffia, and some-times we made them with stripes of coloured raffia. They were very useful under vases. We also made serviette rings. We did not find these so useful. Not many of us used serviettes.

As we improved however, we put this work to good use. straw hats were very fashionable at this time and it was possible to buy them in an untrimmed state. With a border embroidery pattern, and coloured raffia we sewed through the paper all around the crown. When we had completed the work the paper was carefully pulled away leaving us with a nicely decorated hat. They were very exclusive too, because no two girls did exactly the same pattern, or colour scheme.

It was about this time that work was very scarce. Lots of men were out of work. I suppose it must of been due to the General strike. During the winter some of the children were having to come to school without any breakfast. It was obvious too that their clothing was totally inadequate during the cold weather, and their shoes were practically non-existent. Soon it 'was a regular occurrence after morning assembly for the teacher to ask the children to step forward if their father was out of work. They were given some food, and strong boots were issued to them, courtesy I think, of the Birmingham Post and Mail, when necessary. I remember how I cried when I stepped forward one morning because Dad had been out of a job for a week. Out teacher then was Miss. Timmins, she lived across Tippity Green, and she knew us well. She guessed that the reason for Dad being out of work was the frosty weather we were having, and I resumed my seat in class very relieved. I had never worn boots, and I had cried because I thought that I would have to wear them, and also because I felt grieved when I saw little thin legs chafed red and sore with the strong leather.

One thing we did look forward to at this school was our Sports Day. We used to go to Habberley Valley in a charabanc. A rare treat for all of us. Some mothers came along too. We climbed and rambled and played games, and then our tea was served at long tables in the open air tea rooms. We ran our races on the flat floor of the valley. Egg and spoon races, obstacle races, sack races, etc. all accompanied by the cheering shouts of our fellow class members. The winners were all presented with small prizes, pens, pencils, pretty hair slides and such. We all came back tired to death, but all agreeing that Habberley Valley was a little bit of heaven.

In the meantime, our lessons continued in a regular pattern. We gradually got used to learning poems, sometimes quite long ones, and reciting them to the rest of the class. I liked poetry myself. I liked the rhythm and the alliteration. I also liked reading the very long ones in class, and learning some of the well known passages by heart, including some of Shakespeare too. I'm afraid this enjoyment was not shared by all of the class.

One day I went with some of the other children to the Board School at Blackheath. We walked down from Hawes Lane, across the fields by the Labour Club, and down Ross; and we sat the examination for Wright's Lane Secondary School. At the ordinary schools, we left at fourteen, at Grammar schools the children stayed until they were sixteen, and at Secondary schools Commercial subjects were taught, and they left school at fifteen. In spite of the fact that I was under age I passed the examination. Benny Round was the only one besides me, and he left our school to attend Wright's Lane. I didn't go. Mr. Hopcroft had entered me for the examination in preparation for the Grammar School examination, later to be known as the 11-plus. Barbara and Mary Hopcroft both went to Dudley Girl's High School and I hoped that eventually I would go there too. But unfortunately Dad had other ideas. He would not hear of me having any homework, and he told Mr. Hopcroft that even if I passed the examination he would on no account let me attend the Grammar School. I grieved over it for a very long time, but I got over it eventually, I think.

Sewing lessons were going well by now. We were about ten years old and were learning to make simple clothes. Underclothes usually with a run and fell seam, and then we were taught how to make Magyar style dresses with French seams. We had a choice of Pink or Blue, trimmed with white around the neck and sleeves. The school did not boast a sewing machine. The teacher at that time was Miss. Furber and I shall always remember her because she taught us how to make 'Thrift Garments'. I took a striped cotton poplin shirt of Dad's that was torn at the front and would have been difficult to repair. We had to unpick the garment, and then press the pieces out flat so that it was easier to see how much material was available, and the best way of using it up. It was decided that the back of the shirt would make me a pinafore, the good part of the front made the strings, and the sleeves made the pockets. It was a very useful lesson to learn; now before discarding anything I always look at it closely to see whether I think I could make another garment out of it. During the War this was most useful. Clothes could only be purchased if you had the necessary clothing coupons, so I made skirts out of Dad's trousers and pinafore dresses out of Mom's coats. Washed and turned suiting looked quite new.

With only four teachers, including Mr. Hopcroft, and only four classrooms, the teachers had to be flexible. The lessons always had to cover a broad range. Unlike modern schools where pupils are graded by age, and by talent, mostly we had two grades, or standards, as we called them in each classroom. The left half would be standard three for instance, and the right half standard four. In each case there would be an upper and a lower level of intellect, to say nothing of the in-betweens. Somehow they managed to weld the whole lot together when necessary to make one whole class, and to split it up again into little groups, or even at times to single individuals, so that each child was able to progress at their own pace, occasionally staying in a standard for two years, or missing a standard altogether and advancing into the next class. This required very skillful handling by the teachers; more skill I think than having a class all more or less at the same level.

Standard “four was one of the classes that I skipped. I went into Standard Five, which was one of Mr. Hopcroft’s classes, before I was ten years old. I was the youngest child in this section. It comprised Standards Five, Six, and Seven. I think there were three boys in the top grade. Alf Cole, Fred Horton, and Fred Willetts. Because everyone else was older than I was, Monday was an awkward day for me. All the girls went to Siviter’s Lane school for Cookery and Laundry lessons, and the boys went there too on Monday mornings for Woodwork classes. Because of this I was alone; so I became teacher’s monitor for the first half hour, and then I sat with Standard Four for the rest of the morning. When the boys returned for the afternoon I joined in with their arithmetic lessons. including Algebra, which normally the girls did not do.

The boys had a football team, and eventually the girls had a netball pitch laid out in the playground. I played wing, but I am not very sports minded, indeed I could even say I am not bothered with sport of any kind one iota. The boys of course were always playing football or cricket, in their playground, but I always think one of the best uses we made of the playground was playing leapfrog. After school had finished for the day we often played leapfrog. Boys and girls together, young and old. We made a very large border all round the girl’s playground. with such a diversity of ages and sizes it was funny to see the big boys crouching down on all fours for the little ones to jump, when they in turn had to stand upright while the bigger children took a leap right over their heads.

There was one other use made of our playground which I could never enjoy - Drawing. Against the rear wall we used to line up with pencil and paper at the ready. The view was beautiful.. To our left were the Walton and Clent Hills, in front, on the horizon, the Clee Hills, and on clear days, away to our right, the Wrekin. Halesowen, Cradley Heath, Old Hill, and Netherton, were in the foreground below us. Most of the other children managed to get the horizon down on paper. I never did very well. No matter how long I held out my arm, and squinted along my pencil, I never could manage to get my perspective right.

When one is happy doing something time seems to go by very quickly. So the months had rapidly slipped into years, and suddenly it was 1929. Our school was to close down and all the pupils were to be dispersed to other local schools. All the boys aged eleven and over were to go the new school in Britannia Road, and all the girls aged eleven and over, and that would include me, were to report to Siviter’s Lane, no longer to be a mixed school, but now to be called Siviter’s Lane Senior Girls School, after the long holiday.

One of the advantages of attending a small school I had found, was the fact that the teachers got to know each child personally. They knew our parents, and often other relatives too. Family background, and present living conditions. They were aware of the children who had a paper round, who had to take dinners, and the children who had to hurry home to help mind younger brothers and sisters, or even sick mothers sometimes. This knowledge must have been useful to the teachers too. It must have explained at times work that fell below standard, when times were difficult at home. It also meant that they were fully aware of the pupils who did not have any responsibilities - then the shirkers would catch out. The cane was used quite often in those days, and six of the best was often awarded for serious misdemeanour. Lesser offences carried whacks across the palms of the hands. Mostly however we were given 'lines' to learn. This was usually an apt passage from Shakespeare for the older children. Writing lines in the form of 'I must not do' was considered a complete waste of time. To learn a passage from the Bible, a chapter, or a Psalm, was constructional, and therefore more worthwhile, it was also better than detention.

When I see the large numbers of pupils at some of the modern schools, and know that the teachers can never know intimately all the pupils with whom they come into contact I think of the small village schools and I wonder whether despite the modern equipment they are such an improvement after all.

Even Siviter's Lane School was not large if one compares it to a modern comprehensive school, but it certainly looked large to us on our first morning there. Mom had attended this school since it had first opened. Of course it was a mixed school with separate entrances for boys and girls. I remember standing in the Hall that first morning making comparisons. The Hall itself seemed to be as big as our old school, and several doors that I could see opened into the various classrooms. When we had had our Morning Assemblies we had simply to stand in our places at our desks, and all turn to face Mr. Hopcroft. The curtains were slid open, but not the central partition, and when the final hymn had been sung the curtains were closed again and everyone was ready to begin the days work. Now we were to stand in classes, and at the end of Assembly we were to file off to our classrooms to the accompaniment of a march playing upon a gramophone.

We learned that the classes were now to be known as 'Forms' instead of Standards. 'C' was for first year pupils, 'B' Second year, and 'A' for the Third year. As we left school at fourteen in those days, this was of course, the final year. Each year was sub-divided according to ability. so we had '1C' for top grade, '2C' for second grade and '3C' for lower grade, and so on, with '1A' being the top form in the school. As each person's name was called out so was the form number so that we knew which classroom to go to. I was sent to '1C'.

Although the girls came from several different schools they were not all strangers. Some of the girls had been at Currall Road Infants and were local children, some attending our Sunday School too. One of the girls I was happy to meet again was Minnie Brinton from Bell End. We had been in the same class at infant school and neither of us could roll our 'R's'. After a little while, when the class had sorted itself out, we began to share a desk again at the front of the class, and we continued to do so until the day we left.

Another big change now in our school life was having a different teacher for different subjects. Not that we were chasing about to different classrooms, wasting time, but at the end of each session the teacher would quietly leave the classroom and the next teacher would come in. We also had Form Mistresses, and ours was Miss Thomas. She was Welsh, and she took us for all the English

Subjects and geography. I liked her from the start. The lessons she gave us were interesting. and for me at any rate, made even more interesting by her lovely Welsh lilt. I love nice speaking voices. This was especially appreciated on Friday afternoons; it was the practice then to read a story to the class for the last lesson, and the first story that she read to us was' The Little Princess', and we were all fascinated. No one made any effort to rush home and we all eagerly awaited the continuation of the story the next week. I have read the story myself many times since, and seen it on television, but I still recall Miss. Thomas reading to us best of all. I had never had stories like this read to me before. Without radio and television the only reading that we were likely to hear was on Sundays when the lessons from the Bible were read at Chapel.

This Friday afternoon story reading lasted the whole of the three years I was at Siviter's Lane, and I think we were lucky that we had teachers who could read well and who introduced us to books, and authors, we may not have chosen if left to our own devices. Books like Jerome K. Jeromes's 'Three Men in a Boat' and 'Three Men on the Bummel'. I used to read these to Lesley and Martyn, one chapter per day, and we still think them hilarious.

Poetry too was a favourite English lesson. I am very glad that we used to have to learn a lot of poems off by heart. Poems that today's children never seem to hear about. Grey's 'Elegy', 'The Deserted Village',' Vitae Lampada', 'Casablanca'. and many more from Palgrave's Golden Treasury.

At times, when sleep refuses to come, and I have been lying quietly in bed, these poems have come back to me and I have found great joy in reciting them over to myself. I have been told that men taken prisoner during the way, and especially those kept in solitary confinement, kept themselves sane by reciting poetry learned at school. I can well believe this to be true.

For Arithmetic, History, Hygiene and Nature Study, we had Miss. P. Bennett, probably the strictest teacher in the school, but her health was poor and I always think that may have had a lot to do with it. Our Needlework classes were taken by Miss. Mabel George. She also taught the Primary Class at Sunday School. I had known her all my life and I had never called her anything else but Mabel. It was very strange having to learn to call her Miss. George.

All of these lessons, although more advanced were not new to us, but what was new was Country Dancing. I must admit I had never heard of it before, but I loved it, and with Minnie Brinton as my partner I was ready to go 'Gathering Peascods, or do a 'Shepherds's Hey' at any time. I did not however tell Dad. He would not have liked it. He was very strict, and very strait laced. He really believed that any form of dancing was some form of Devil Worship, so I told Mom, but we never told Dad. It was another fifteen years before he began to mellow.

During that first year we also had another teacher named Mrs. Green. She had I think been widowed quite recently, and she was to be with us for some unspecified reason, temporarily. What I do know however is that we had to write out for her part of a speech from Shakespeare's 'Hamlet', 'The Advice of Polonius to His Son'. I still have the original bit of paper, and never forget the advice to us to live up to it. In case you have never read it yourselves, it goes like this:

Give thy thoughts no tongue,
Nor any unproportion'd thought his act.
Be thou familiar, but by no means vulgar.
The friends thou hast, and their adoption tried,
Grapple them to thy soul with hoops of steel;
But do not dull thy palm with entertainment
Of each new-hatched, unfledged comrade.
Beware Of entrance to a quarrel; but, being in'
Bear't that the opposed may beware of thee.
Give every man thine ear, but few thy voice;
Take each man's censure, but reserve thy judgment.
Costly thy habit as thy purse can buy,
But not expressed in fancy; rich, not gaudy;
For the apparel oft proclaims the man;
Neither a borrower or a lender be;
For loan oft loses both itself and friend;
And borrowing dulls the edge of husbandry.
This above all, - to thine own self be true;
And it must follow, as the night the day,
Thou canst not then be false to any man.

I think this advice is as true today as when William Shakespeare first wrote it.

Any change of school can be upsetting, and the first year is not particularly easy. The second year is much different. Examinations have taken place, and we know which form we shall be in before the September break. A batch of eleven year olds arrive at the school, and now they are the juniors and we are the old hands. We have moved across the Hall to a new classroom, and a new Form Mistress, Miss. Spencer in charge of Form 'IB'.

I continued to make good progress in all subjects, except Drawing of course, but I enjoyed the Handwork section very much. These lessons were held in the Practical Room. This was an out-building in the playground, the Laundry was on the ground floor, just as it always had been, and the upper floor, which was entered by a stone staircase from the 'boy's' playground, had once been the Woodwork room. I spent many happy hours in there working. My reports may not have been glowing perhaps, but, although my free-hand drawing was never likely to improve, I found I was better with a compass and ruler, and I had quite a good eye for colour. I liked stencilling and making patterns with a cut potato, or small pieces of cut cane. We learned how to repair books, putting new corners with cardboard and binder's cloth. We repaired the school hymn books and bibles this way, sometimes putting on whole new covers, and making our own end-papers with Indian ink in water to get a marbled effect.

Also using Indian ink, we learned to do Old English printing. We used this for making calendars and name plates. I found I was quite good at this too much to my delight, it helped to compensate for my awful drawings. Of course we made other things too. Sea-grass stools, portfolios, with shiny leather effect outsides, and lining papers which we had designed and made ourselves. We painted and beaded cork mats: and to learn Appliqué work we made ourselves a work box. These were made in sections: a base, a lid, and six or eight sections for the sides. Cardboard padded and covered with material, inside and outside, then stitched together. I remember that mine was Brown Holland cloth on the outside, and orange cotton on the inside. I appliquéd three oranges, and three green leaves on the lid. Padded inside for a pin cushion, and it fastened with a loop and button. They may not have won any prizes, but they were very serviceable and I used mine until it wore out.

Perhaps I found it so very useful because I did quite a bit of sewing. Some of this we did in the Practical Room too. The long sturdy tables were ideal for cutting out, and for the sewing machine. The cupboards held the rolls of cloth. Besides calico, which we used for making pillow and bolster cases, we had rolls of gingham, and 'Bo-peep' prints, at fourpence and sixpence per yard. Note that this is in old money. Out of this we used to make our own dresses. I was used to a treadle machine at home, but at school we had two hand machines. I never found them as convenient as a treadle because one hand was always kept busy with the handle.

We started off with plain sewing, naturally. This was where pillow cases came in, very useful for learning to sew long straight seams. Then in those days they were fastened with button and buttonholes, the so-called 'housewife' style had not yet come in, so we had to learn to sew buttons on firmly, and to work button-holes. All the girls wore long black woolen stockings, so we had to learn to darn properly. Remember we had learned how to weave bits of coloured paper at the Infant School, and Raffia work at Hawes Lane. Well nothing learned is ever wasted, it can always be adapted for use later on, just like this.

We never had to make a sampler like the poor children of an earlier age, but as we learned each new skill, we made a little sample on a piece of white cloth or flannel, and they were gradually added to to make a kind of book. There was a square ended button-hole, and a round-ended buttonhole, blanket stitch, chain stitch, faggot stitch, hemming, and cross stitch, and a bit of drawn thread work, with hem-stitch. We did shell-stitch for trimming necks and armholes of underslips, and scallop edges, using a penny, or a half-penny to draw them in first, for a variety of trimmings. We made a pretty cover for these books and kept them for later reference.

On Monday mornings we had Domestic Science subjects. We were divided into two groups, taking Cookery and Laundry alternately. One group having Miss. Worthing as teacher and one group having Miss. Broadbent. Of Miss. Worthing I can say very little, not being my teacher I doubt if I said more than half a dozen words to her in three years. I do remember that she had a very nice voice. One day as a special treat she came to our classroom and sang for us some

Welsh songs and I remember her singing 'Land of my Fathers'.

Miss Broadbent I shall never forget. I was glad when I knew that I was to be in her group because when Mom and Aunt Martha first went to Siviter's Lane, when it opened, Miss. Broadbent was there, and she taught them. She was very tall and thin. Victorian in appearance and manner. A strict disciplinarian; she stood no nonsense from any of us, but was not sneering or sarcastic. We all stood in awe of her, but speaking for my own class I don't think any of us were afraid of her. If we did wrong, we stood rebuked, but we knew the rebuke was justified. If she ever spoke tongue in cheek, there was usually a glint in the *eye.* I don't believe I ever heard her laugh outright, a smile, a stifled chuckle perhaps, but yet we knew she had a sense of humour. One felt she had schooled herself, as well as her scholars, to behave decorously in class. Although her manner appeared brusque, she was kindly at heart, although stern, a reprimand was usually given in private, behind the range, rather than in front of the class.

She would talk to us sometimes of Mrs. Beeton, and tell us of extravagant recipes for elaborate dishes, but the things she taught us were practical and economical. She always said anybody without sense could feed a family if they had unlimited supplies, but to feed a family properly on a normal man's wage called for real skill. The housewife needed to be both practical and thrifty, and to learn to shop wisely, and keep within a budget. What we were like as pupils then, it is very difficult to say, but her teaching certainly lasts down the years. I think of her when I stack soap to harden, measure soap powder into the washer, or even beat an egg. It is said the proof of the pudding is in the eating; the proof of her good teaching is in the fact that it is still remembered and acted upon, sometimes perhaps subconsciously, she was a great lady.

In the summer, when the weather was hot, we had some lessons outside in the playground. The Siviter's Lane corner had been planted with a few trees, probably when the school was first opened, and was always called, rather grandly, 'The Plantation'. There were two or three winding paths, some shrubs, and a few oases of grassy patches. On a suitable patch we would sit down, armed with text books, notebooks and pencils, facing the teacher who sat on a chair.

Nature study was a favourite subject taken out of doors. Birds, bees, and butterflies, all had their place in our plantation. The bees would bumble about busily from flower to flower, and not bother us at all. The butterflies would linger sometimes, alighting on or near to us, so that we could really see them. The birds however regarded our visits as an intrusion. The blackbirds especially liked to callout warnings to us pretty often. After all we were invading their privacy. The plantation was their territory.

The sunlight filtering through the leaves, making an ever changing pattern on faces and arms, as the breeze gently moved the leaves on the lower branches of the trees. High up in the topmost branches there was always a curious swishing noise as the wind played through the tops of the trees. I think those trees really liked the children. They were like a choir singing quietly in the background. Shutting out the noises from beyond the school wall, but joining in with us as we quietly did our lessons, occasionally relaying back to us the muted sound of the gramophone as some other class did country dancing on the level part of the playground.

They always sounded different at night. Then, as we walked past the wall the wind soughed through the branches and made melancholy, lonely sounds; spooky and miserable.

Sometimes the shafts of sunlight would beam through the boughs, highlighting a section of bush, or a clump of wild flowers, like a giant spotlight upon a stage, especially in the late afternoon when the sun began to get lower in the sky. I can recall Miss. Winnie Bennett had a beautiful brooch with a large stone in the centre, and sometimes, when a shaft of sunlight caught it, all the colours of the spectrum were mirrored back to us. It was like being caught at the end of the rainbow. This used to happen in the classroom too. Then the lights would dance over the walls and ceiling. I'm sure if one of them had spoken and announced that she was tinkerbell, I for one would not have been surprised.

All of this may sound as though I was day-dreaming throughout the lessons, but this is not true. I was attentive enough at the time, but one's other senses were working overtime too, and upon reflection, these senses also recall what they saw and felt. In the same way that one can recall the sound of chalk squeaking on a blackboard, or the restless shuffling of feet under desks, if the class became inattentive. Neither sound happened all the time, they are just sounds associated with school, that form a kaleidoscope and come back unbidden to the mind as a composite whole, and help us to re-establish the feelings we had once a long time ago.

After the holiday in 1931 I had moved up to the top class 'lA'. Our Form Mistress now was to be Miss. George. Although the lessons appeared to carry on normally there was a slightly disjointed feeling to them. I think now it must have been a kind of restlessness in certain quarters which pervaded the atmosphere. As each child reached the age of fourteen they were allowed to leave at the end of that term, and not wait for the end of the school year, so I think this must have given them a touch of the 'don't cares' which perhaps was a bit unsettling for the rest of us. The class of course got less and less at the end of each term.

Besides the teachers that I have mentioned, there were others of course, but as I have said before, if they did not take our particular class, then, in most cases we saw very little of them except in assembly. There was Miss. Dimmock, she took us for a short while for P.E.; Miss. Hickman, a newcomer to the school just before I left; Miss. Eld, from Dudley; I think she only took us on very rare occasions as far as I remember. Last but by no means least, was the Headmistress, Miss. Sarah Harrison. She came from Old Hill, was strict and authorative, and we stood in awe of her. We saw her in the hall for Morning Assembly, and occasionally she came to the classrooms for various reasons. To be sent to see her when one had committed an offence against any of the school regulations was never taken lightly, and she was quite handy with the cane if it was needed, which fortunately, was only on rare occasions. But she was fair, and always ready to listen to reason before passing judgment.

When we were in our last year we had far more to do with her as she took some of our classes herself. Then what a shock we had! Although one would never have taken any liberties, we found her very friendly indeed. She talked to us, often at great length, on a variety of subjects which were new and strange to us. She had a great fund of anecdotes, and she also told us of visits which she had made to the continent which amazed us in 1932. Apart from the men who had been abroad with the Army and Navy, few of us had ever met anyone who had been abroad. Some had relatives abroad, as we had in America, but they had emigrated; not a holiday, where you went to Germany, France, or Switzerland, and then came back. Then it all seemed as remote to us as going to the moon. It broadened our outlook, and brought us into contact with real people in real places, instead of just names on a map. She had a perky sense of humour, which I particularly, enjoyed, as she related to us adventures which had happened to her, and her friends, when they had been abroad.

She talked to us of opera, which most of us had scarcely heard of, and she read to us the complete story of Wagner's 'Ring' operas, and she talked to us also of the Passion Play at Oberammergau which had taken place in 1930. I dreamed of visiting the place myself but it was to be another forty years before it came true. She helped to round off our education by encouraging us to discuss things with her, and to ask her questions. To me she seemed a tower of strength, and I know she always tried to help me when she could.

My last day at school came when we broke up for the September holidays. I said reluctant farewell to all my teachers and to friends, and went home to cry my eyes out.

WORK, WAR, AND WEDDINGS

The only bright spot as far as I could tell about 1932 was the advent into our lives of a wireless set. I had been given money on Monday mornings with which to buy National Savings Stamps, which could be exchanged in due course for National Savings Certificates. After I left school these were cashed and we set off to Blackheath to Priest's shop in the Market Place. I believe Dad used to play football with Mr. Priest so we went there for his advice. The days of the old cat's whisker and earphones era was now over and we became the proud possessors of an Osram 4 Valve Superhet. We thought it was marvellous. The Accumulator had to be taken to Tibbetts' shop to be charged but we found it better than the gramophone. We had some nice records but of course it had to be wound up and the needle had to be changed all the time. Now the announcer talked to us and besides the music we heard the news too. We really thought we had Entertainment with a capital E, right in our own home.

We used to have the "Birmingham Gazette" which Dad used to read after tea at night. Usually I only skimmed through it looking at the headlines and the pictures. I used to have "The Children's Newspaper" which came out weekly, and in fact I continued to have it long after I was married. Any news which I considered important I could read in that. I read of the Great Hunger Strike, and the Opening of the Sydney Harbour Bridge, and the Shakespeare Memorial Theatre at Stratford on Avon. Jim Mollinson and Amy Johnson, now Mrs. Mollinson, had both broken air records and Malcolm Campbell drove Blue Bird at 253 m.p.h.

Of great interest to us was the uniting of the Wesleyan Methodist Groups, to be known now as the Methodist Church. Eventually we had to have new Hymn Books at Chapel. Grandad Hodgetts was taken ill and died in November.

Away on the horizon the proverbial small clouds were gathering. Oswald Mosley founded the British Union of Fascists, and in Germany the Nazi Party gained a majority in the Reichstag.

In America F.D.R. Roosevelt became President for the first time. I have no doubt I was more interested in the fact that Walt Disney did his first silly Symphony.

When I had left school behind me I was completely bewildered. There were no careers advisors available in those days. Dad. had offered me the choice of learning tailoring, or I could go and learn Shorthand/Typing somewhere. I felt between the devil and the deep blue sea. Although I had been used to making my own cotton frocks and doing plain sewing of various kinds, both by hand and sewing machine, the thought of sewing all day and every day appalled me. Shorthand/Typing was an enigma I couldn't solve. I simply didn't know anything about it, and I suppose I was afraid of failing at something that Dad had had to pay for me to learn. With no one to advise me I stayed put, and hoped that I could go to Evening Classes in the autumn, and maybe I could learn something there that would be useful.

Granny Hadley had always said, "They'm frightened to let the wind blow on thee," also being known as hob-reared, and I suppose I had been over-protected. Never-the-less Mom took me on the train to Birmingham the next Thursday to look for work. Enquiries had been made locally but there were no vacancies. The 1930's were years of unemployment the same as the 1980's.

We went first to Typhoo Tips Tea. A lot of questions were asked and answered, then I was told that there were no vacancies at the moment but they would bear me in mind. There was no hint as to the length of time involved so we went to Goldbergs where they made soft toys. On the way back we stopped at the ticket office and bought my first season ticket (eight shillings in old money) for one month. Next day I began work.

I was used to getting up early so that I could read before going to school, so getting ready for work was never a problem. Of course it was light when I first started work but as Autumn advanced so the mornings became darker. It was lovely watching the stars fading in the sky, and the earth changing from misty grey to green as the sun began to rise above the house tops.

There used to be crowds of people converging on to the station at Blackheath. I often used to wonder where they all went. Some, like me, were new to work. The boys especially, showed it. At school they had had to wear short trousers, and when they began work, unless there was a younger brother of convenient size to hand them down to, they went to work with their short trousers on. Nobody minded. It was a custom to which we were all familiar. So, no long trousers until the short ones were worn out. It used to be quite an occasion when a boy had his first suit with long trousers.

Aunt Martha and Mirrie Parsons travelled on the same train although they had to get a tram to Aston after getting off the train at Snow Hill station.

My first task when I began work was testing the growls for Teddy Bears. If there was no growl when they were turned over they were discarded. Eventually I was given fabric skins to stuff with wood-wool to make a little animal. When these were satisfactorily stuffed they went to the trimming department where they were given eyes and bows of ribbon. It looked much more exciting than stuffing them. It was very interesting to see the materials being smoothed out and a huge pattern laid on top, pressed down hard before the sharp cutter was guided round the pattern cutting out hundreds in various colours all at the same time.

After two weeks Marjorie Page came to say Typhoo had a vacancy if I was still interested, so Mom told me to give in my notice and go to work there, then I should have someone to travel with in the winter.

Typhoo was a 'family' firm. sir John Sumner was a caring man. The older employees who had been with the firm from the beginning were known to him by their Christian names. When he walked around he would speak to each of them, and if anyone of us needed help or advice, his office door was open to all. On special occasions, like Armistice Day, 'we had our own little service led by Sir John. I think he was respected by us all.

I duly presented myself the next week and began to learn to pack tea. Packing tea in those days was done by hand on an everlasting-belt system. One girl opened the white paper bag, another girl pushed it on to the funnel and a quarter pound of tea dropped into it. She in turn placed the packet on to the belt where the next four girls took a packet in turn and 'turned-in' the white paper bag. Any advertising matter, and a stiffener, were held in place with the left hand while putting the outer box on with the right hand. These were returned to the belt, and further down the line three more girls gummed the bases of the boxes and added gummed paper seals to the top. Finally, the last girl took out twenty packets and parcelled them into five pound parcels before stacking them on to a platform. When 1,000 pounds was thus stacked the platform was wheeled away to the Dispatching Department, and an empty platform put into position ready to start all over again. Each machine turned out about thirty packets per minute so one needed to be deft.

The work was not difficult after practice but like all repetitive work it could become rather dulling to the senses.

I had been looking forward to going to Evening Classes at school but to no avail. We had to begin to work overtime for one hour until six-thirty. The next train was at seven-twenty so I could not get home until after eight. Too late to go to classes.

To overcome any boredom, we used to tell one another stories, either books that we had read, or a film. For the last two years or so I had been going to the 'Pavilion' in Blackheath High street on Saturday afternoons to the children's matinees. It was one penny at the front and two pence at the rear. Because I used to have "The Children's Newspaper' and "Schoolgirl's Weekly" I only had one penny to spend so if I wanted to go to the pictures I used to have to do extra errands and jobs. Clean all the knives and forks with 'Glitto' They were not stainless steel in those days. The E.P.N.S. ones had to be cleaned with silver polish. Wash all the bottles, and then bottle the home-made porter, or lemonade. Polish every ones shoes etcetera. Somehow I usually managed, and off I would run down Ross to join the queue. Every week we saw part of a serial and it always went off when either the hero, or the heroine was in a dreadfully tight spot, so we had to go to see how they managed to escape.

I must admit I was very surprised when I went to work to find some of the girls went four times every week. Now that I was fourteen I had to pay at least sixpence in the 'King's', ninepence in the rear. Out of my 10 shillings a week wages I only had one shilling pocket money to last me. Of course in those days we not only saw the main film and the news. There was also a "B" picture, a cartoon, a short feature, adverts and film trailers, and in some cases a cinema organ recital in some cinemas. Not forgetting a short live interlude on stage, usually something appropriate to the film being shown. For instance when we saw the film 'Smilin' Through' a man sang the song on stage.

Someone had usually been to see a film the night before and was quite prepared to regale us with full details. I didn't know much about film stars then. The only one I really knew was Ramon Navarro because I saw him in 'Ben Hur", otherwise I was more interested in Rin-Tin-Tin.

Twice each week our positions were changed so that we each did our stint of the different jobs. Sometimes too we were changed to half-pound packing lines. Occasionally also there would be special export lines to pack. Greaseproof paper liners, and each packet cellophane wrapped. The biggest difficulty of course on the everlasting belt system is in not being able to leave one's place. It is impossible to go to the toilet, or go anywhere else for that matter without the girl who was 'over the line' taking over one's job. I have no idea whether this still goes on in places of employment. I have no one to ask.

I have already mentioned the Dispatching Department where customer's orders were attended to, but of course before tea can be packed and dispatched it had to be delivered in bulk. This I always found very interesting. In fact, the story of tea makes fascinating reading. I tried to find out as much as I could. The more one knows and understands about a subject the more interesting it becomes. Below the packing room floor was the Bonded Warehouse, and we had our own branch of the canal. The tea was delivered direct from the ships to canal barges, and then up to us. The bargees would manoeuvre the chests on to a stacker which lifted them up from water level to drop them on to gravity rollers. From there they were stacked on to platforms, and stored, after being checked by the Customs and Excise Men, until required. Ceylon Tea then came in nice oblong chests of uniform size, but Indian tea came in a variety of sizes and weights. The names of the tea gardens were stencilled on the sides. We had great fun sometimes trying to pronounce the names which were often very long. These were always known as London Blend, probably because they had been purchased at the London Tea Auctions.

Christmas came and soon it was 1933. We had an outing from work to Whipsnade Zoo, recently opened. Later on I went with Aunt Martha and Emmie Baker to Rhyl on holiday. It was the first time I had been to the seaside for a week.

Malcolm Campbell had increased his speed to 272 m.p.h.. Walt Disney made Three Little Pigs and Alexander Korda made the Private Lives of Henry the Eighth. We didn't know it, but the little clouds had grown a bit bigger. Germany left the League of Nations. Adolph Hitler was appointed Chancellor of Germany. The Reichstag was burned and the Communists were blamed. Concentration Camps were started.

During 1934 we moved house. Mucklows were building houses in Park Avenue and Mom and I would have been pleased to move into one, but Dad decided not to have one of these modern ones but to move to Hawes Lane, because he considered them to be better built. There were two houses for sale, one with vacant possession. Dad bought that one and Uncle Jack Southall bought the other as an investment property. Mrs. Clifford lived in that one. They were the centre two of four villas known as St Giles Terrace. They had a bay window to the front room. The front door led to a hall which opened out into a square with the stairs on the left, and beneath the stairs and down three steps, the pantry. A further flight of stone steps led to a dry cellar. I'm afraid I'm not much for cellars. In the twenty years I lived there you could count on one hand the times I ventured down there. There was a row of hooks on the right hand wall of this square for hanging outdoor clothes. A small window inset in the wall overlooking the living-room beyond brought in daylight, as did a glass fanlight over the front door. The living room was large. The width of the front room and the hall combined. The back door opened on to a blue-brick paved yard. A good sized scullery was detached from the house which contained brick built boiler, half range grate and baking oven. A path at the side led to a coal house, an extension of the scullery. Separate from this was the flush toilet, and what had been the ash pit now housed the dustbin. Upstairs was a large square landing; to the right a bedroom over the front room, to the left a bedroom over part of the living room and a second bedroom over part of the living room and the entry which was shared with the house next door. They in turn had a room which extended over their hall and the entry.

As soon as we were settled in we lost no time in making our way to the Gas showrooms in Birmingham Road, Blackheath, to choose a new gas cooker. Up until then almost all of our cooking had been done on the open fire, using either saucepans, cooking pots, or the stew-jar. Our Sunday joint was roasted in the oven. We never used a meat jack, but small pieces of meat, chops, or rashers of bacon or sausages would be cooked in front of the fire using a Dutch Oven, commonly known as a toaster, which rested on strides. These were iron legs hinged at the top and having hooks which fastened on to the bars at the front of the fire, so really the food was grilled.

It was very hot in the summer having to keep the fire going for cooking and boiling water for tea. That was one reason why lots of people sat on the doorsteps, or at least in the doorways in the summer. We had been luckier than some, we had used a square block contraption in our back kitchen. It was a cube about a foot square. The gas jet was on a swivel allowing the jet to be turned to grill meat underneath, with enough heat to keep a saucepan simmering on top, or a kettle, but of course it wasn't big enough to cook for a family, but it did mean that most days in the summer we could let our fire out after the dinner was cooked, and boil the kettle on the gas; but we had never had a gas cooker. Now we had a "Newhome" fitted in the back kitchen and the heat of the oven could be regulated properly when we made cakes instead of throwing in bits of paper to test whether it was still too hot.

Best of all, we did not need to sit out on the step either to keep cool. We had a long garden at the back with panoramic views right out to the Clee Hills, and the sun shone until the last possible moment before slowly sinking away below the horizon.

The Mersey Tunnel was opened in Liverpool by King George the Fifth. William Beebe descended more than half a mile in his Bathysphere. Times here were very hard. The terrible Means Test came into operation and succeeded in thoroughly demorolising the working classes. Over in Germany President Hindenburg died and Adolf Hitler became Reichfuhrer.

From Typhoo we went to Blackpool for the day by Special Train, with Lunch served on the way there and High Tea served on the return journey. It was the first time that I had dined on a train and I must admit I still love it.

The next two years brought very disquieting news. Italy invaded Abyssinia. The news reels at the cinemas were terrible. In Germany the Persecution of the Jews began.

The Silver Jubilee Train ran at 112 m.p.h. and we celebrated the Silver Jubilee of King George and Queen Mary. The King however was not well and in January he died. Regular broadcasting was suspended and an announcer stated somberly, 'the King's life is drawing to a close'. We walked about with black armbands and bunches of mauve or purple flowers pinned to our coats and there were great crowds in the streets in Birmingham.

The Prince of Wales ascended the throne, to be known as King Edward the Eighth. When he was younger everyone had had high hopes but these had been replaced by grave doubts owing to his association with the twice divorced American Wallis Simpson.

Spain began a civil War, with Hitler and Mussolini supporting the Rebels and Russia and other Communists supporting the Government. The Italians captured Addis Ababa, eventually Haile Selaise came to England.

The Crystal Palace was destroyed by fire. Television was begun at Alexander Palace. The S.S. Queen Mary made her maiden voyage and she gained the Blue Riband.

In Germany the Eleventh Olympiad was held. Herr Hitler was not pleased that the American coloured athlete Jesse Owens, beat his Aryans, and they succeeded in re-occupying the Rhineland without any Allied protest.

Perhaps we were too busy with our own affairs. Things came to a head between King and Parliament. The King, who was never to be crowned, abdicated. A former Duke of York, his brother George, became King in his stead.

We had electricity installed at No. 48.

In 1937 Walt Disney launched Snow White and the Seven Dwarfs. The first full length feature cartoon. We loved it. Korda made Elephant Boy with Sabu, and the uncrowned King, now known as the Duke of Windsor, married Wallis Simpson. He was very much put out because she became a Duchess but not a Royal one. Council re-housing was well under way and Dad left private housing to go to work for Oldbury Direct Labour.

King George and Queen Elizabeth were crowned on the twelfth of May, but a couple of weeks before that Typhoo and I parted company and I went to work with Aunt Martha at Buttons Ltd, Aston. They were I believe the largest button manufacturing firm in the world, at that time anyway. They had large rambling premises on both sides of the road. I was in the 'closing' shop, and amongst other things, like blazer buttons, and buttons for such diverse things as dresses and mattresses, they made buttons from horn and bone and something we called erinoid, a kind of vegetable I believe, which had to be sliced, of course this was before plastic.

We also made military buttons. The instruction cards which came with the order gave very precise information regarding the gauge and type of metal to be used, and the exact weight of each button on completion. No paper liners were ever allowed in British military buttons. I made many gross of these for all regiments, and the R.A.F.

I never went all over the factory, unfortunately, but it was thrilling to go through the cutting shops, and see, and hear! the large machines cutting the blanc discs out of the rolls of metal, and the stamping shop where the shells had the design stamped on them. When they had been through the acid bath and barrelled they came to us all shiny and bright. The British Government announced are-armament programme, and we began to work overtime on Saturday afternoons.

I went with a friend to stay in Torquay for a week. No coach this time, we went by train. It was a pleasure to see the stations in those days. Lovely colourful flower beds. hanging baskets, and everything tidy, clean and bright.

Perhaps we couldn't be blamed for trying to cling to our youth. We certainly saw in the news-reels at the cinema enough to scare us and to warn us of the troubles to come. We knew that the war clouds were looming larger. With Italy still waging war against Abyssinia, brother fighting against brother in Spain and in Germany we saw the massing of Hitler's followers with their flags with the twisted swastika making a fearsome sight. There was even war in the Far East between China and Japan. In March Hitler annexed Austria. Neville Chamberlain flew three times to Germany finally returning waving a bit of paper and saying 'Peace in our time', but it had a hollow ring. The Munich Agreement as it was called, wasn't worth the paper it was written on. It only served to lull the nation into a false sense of security. Six months later Hitler showed his own contempt of it by marching into Czechoslovakia. By now he had taken over command of the German Army, and following upon his close friendship with Mussolini came the first intimations of anti-Jewish measures in Italy.

We blindly carried on as usual. Going to work, studying the latest fashions, and going to the pictures. Leslie Howard made Pygmalion, and Charlie Chaplin made Modern Times. On the stage, Emlyn Williams scored a hit with the Corn is Green, also starring Dame Sybil Thorndike.

Winston Churchill repeatedly warned the Government of the impending trouble, but he was labelled 'War-monger' for his pains. Even though we knew that the Germans were busily re-arming. Pictures of his storm Troopers armed for battle, and tanks and armoured vehicles on parade showed that while we hoped for peace we too should have been preparing more for the worst - War.

The British Government and France, gave a guarantee to help Poland in case of any foreign aggression. Mussolini invaded Albania. King Zog escaped first to France, then to Britain. In August Hitler signed a pact of friendship with Joseph Stalin. It was a bitter pill to swallow. Hitler was now free to attack Poland knowing that Stalin would not go to her aid.

The civil War ended in Spain. Franco had won. The Government was defeated.

I left Buttons Ltd. at this time and went to work at Firmin's at Hockley. This also was a 'family' firm. Much smaller than Buttons Ltd. but doing similar work. Besides doing military buttons we also made buttons for the new

Auxiliary Fire Service which came into being in 1938. Other departments were also busy making badges both military and private. It is amazing you know how many operations are necessary to turn out a good button, or badge for that matter. I suppose most people never give it a thought, but I can think of about twelve operations:

Shank: Wire cut and shaped.
Back: Blanks cut, shaped, pierced, stamped,
sometimes shank inserted, dipped and barreled.
Shell: Blanks cut, shaped, stamped, dipped and barreled.
Closing shell to back.

Some of the nicest buttons I ever handled were made with real silver coats of arms, and sets of monogrammed blazer buttons in real gold.

One thing I never liked about factory life was the 'lock-out' system. We had to start work at 7.45 a.m. and it was difficult to arrive on time when the train was late, especially in foggy weather, or if there was some delay further back up the line. We used to run from the station, catch a bus, if one came, or run all the way if one didn't, because if the gates were closed we were locked out in the street for thirty minutes. If it happened twice in one week it was for one hour.

Personally I regarded this as most unfair on the train girls. The people who lived close didn't bother to turn up until it was near time to go in when they knew they were late. They had stayed by the fire at home having breakfast, but we had been out of the house about 6.45 a.m. and we had to stand out in the cold and the rain until we were allowed in, sometimes with wet clothes to sit about in all day.

On August the twenty ninth I became twenty-one. Everything was now in turmoil. The fears of everyone were now to be realised. Hitler marched on Poland. The whole of the country was on the alert. With money given to me for my birthday we went shopping in Birmingham. Everywhere soldiers and civilians alike were hard at work. Sandbags were being filled by the thousand. Doorways were being covered and windows latticed with sticky paper, to help avoid splinters of glass or shrapnel, during the expected air-raids. The rehearsals for the blackout and children's evacuation were now over. Now it was the real thing. Black-out material was selling like hot cakes and when I arrived home with my purchases and the tales of walking through tunnels of sandbags into the shops, it was to find Dad busy with the sticky tape, and Mom equally busy with the black-out curtains. All windows were to be covered by Saturday the second of September.

On the morning of Sunday the Third of September I was putting the sweeper round in the living room and at 11.15 a.m. I had to switch off for the official announcement by Prime Minister Neville Chamberlain. All the speculation was now over. We were once again at war with Germany.

The air-raids we had all expected to happen immediately didn't come so we at least had time to get used to the black-out. Cinemas and theatres had closed, but eventually they re-opened. We re-arranged our schedules and those of us who lived out of town went to matinees so that we were back home earlier.

There were very few buses after 9.00 p.m. House building was suspended and Air-raid shelters were erected. Vast water tanks for fire fighting began to appear wherever there was space enough. We had queued for gas masks and been issued with Identity Cards, both of which had to be carried at all times.

If travelling had been difficult before, now as we prepared for winter, we soon realised we were in for a bad time. Eventually all names of stations were removed so as to confound any German parachutists who dropped in. This applied to signposts on roads too of course. Railway carriages had a little blue light which made every one look sick and ghastly. Sufficient to find a seat, if you were lucky, but not light enough to read by, or knit by. Window blinds had to be drawn of course to conform to the black-out regulations.

Railway porters could not callout the name of the station, and when the train was crowded it was very hard fighting to get out before the train moved off again. I have known eighteen people in a corridor carriage meant for eight. It was made worse of course by this extra paraphernalia we were all carrying. Our gas-masks and our black-out torches. These torches had masks on so that the light shone downward, only just enough light to show where curbs were, or other obstacles that might impede us. If the light seemed too bright, or if you were swinging it about in any way, A.R.P. officers could stop you to inspect the torch and you were soon told to mask it more. It was not unusual for passengers to alight at the wrong station, usually the one up, or down, the line from their normal stop. It was all very confusing at first, but like everything else, one got used to it.

This winter of the war became known as the 'phony war', because the expected attacks didn't come. A Ministry of Information had been set up and news was doled out to us as the Censor saw fit. We had to remember that 'Careless talk cost lives' and not expect to be told anything which might be of help to the enemy. We tried to read between the lines but of course it was all speculation. We did know however that Russia had also attacked poor Poland and eventually it was partitioned off between Germany and Russia. With Poland now safely out of the way, Russia launched an attack on Finland.

At sea it was a different matter altogether. Immediately war was declared a passenger ship 'Athenia' was sunk in the Atlantic. The German U Boats had been dispersed to strategic positions beforehand and so had the pocket battleships and they were lying in wait for any Allied shipping. Merchant ships bringing vital supplies suffered very heavy losses during the war.

We gradually learned to cope with shortages, rationing, and bad news. Denmark was over-run by the Germans who then attacked Norway. This was not an easy victory for them however. The gallant people fought valiantly and bravely and the Allies gave all the help that they could give, but the distance was too great and eventually had to be withdrawn. King Haakon, his Government, and as many men from the Armed Forces and Merchant Navy as were able, escaped and came to Great Britain to carryon fighting from here.

Neville Chamberlain resigned as Prime Minister and Winston Churchill became Prime Minister instead, forming a Coalition Government. His strong leadership was just what the nation needed. He could only offer us he said 'blood, toil, tears and sweat' but it was like a shot in the arm.

Over on the continent Hitler now launched into the Battle for France. First Holland fell and the Dutch Royal Family were brought here. By the twenty seventh of May, despite fierce fighting, Belgium was defeated and King Leopold had asked for an armistice. The British Expeditionary Force fought their way back to Dunkirk. So began one of the miracles of history.

It was realised by the authorities that help would be needed to take the troops from the beaches and every available boat and ship of every size and shape began to gather at Dover. They set sail for Dunkirk. For nine days they worked, in very calm seas, almost unprecedented, amidst bombing and shelling by the Germans, they lost many ships and lives, but thankfully over 300,000 were saved. Mussolini chose this time to declare war on Great Britain and France. Germany now was able to over-run France who sued for an armistice. Some of course escaped to Great Britain and under General De Gaulle founded the Free French Resistance Movement. The French Navy was disbanded and Hitler said he would not use their Fleet against the Allies. Of course we could not believe this so the British Mediterranean Fleet sunk the majority of them just to make sure.

There was nothing now to stop Germany attacking us. Winston Churchill broadcast his now famous speech where he said 'Let us brace ourselves therefore to our duties, and so bear ourselves that, if the British Empire and its Commonwealth last for a thousand years, men will say "This was their finest hour." We were alone.

Much equipment had been lost during the evacuation from Dunkirk and it was necessary for overtime to be worked in most factories, often round the clock shift work so as to re-equip the Fighting Forces. It was necessary now for volunteers to defend ourselves and not depend upon the regulars. At first they were called Local Defense Volunteers and they had no real weapons to train with, but later they became known as the Home Guard, and they were issued with uniforms, weapons, and ammunition

It was in July that the Luftwaffe began attacking convoys in the Channel. Hurricanes and Spitfires had to fight off attacks by Dorniers and Junkers. Later they attacked airfields and radar posts in the south. On the seventh of September night bombing of London began. The fifteenth of September brought the greatest fight of all. Great waves of bombers attacked the R.A.F. They were but few in number and tired at that, but gallantly they fought back, their numbers depleted, but still doggedly carried on. At last it was over. The 'few' had defeated the many.

Then the Blitz really started in earnest. London was the main target naturally. Night after night the bombers came over. But other cities were bombed badly too. The bombing at Coventry was so intense it gave us a new word in the English language, 'Coventrated'. We could hear the planes going over us in vast waves when Manchester or Liverpool were being bombed. Locally we were very lucky, we only had a few bombs dropped, but Birmingham was badly hit. Girls at work were going home to eat, then whole families were going off to the public Air-raid Shelters. Lots of people had their own "Anderson" or "Morrison" shelters but we had the cellar and the pantry. If anyone was missing the next morning after a raid everyone was quiet as we worked and waited for news. One could feel the relief when the missing person turned up safe and sound. Walking on rubble and broken glass began to be the norm as we wondered which buildings would be left standing after the next raid.

Getting into work was not too bad, it was getting home again that was the trouble. Countless times I have stood on Hockley station as three or more full trains have gone through before I could get on one. After getting off at Blackheath I had to walk to Hawes Lane. Of all the people getting off at the same time no one else seemed to have to go this way and I walked alone. It meant I did not get home until around nine. It was a long day. The only consolation was that on clear moonless nights, the stars were beautiful, and shone brilliantly, a sight not to be seen when street lighting is switched on.

By Christmas Dad had finished building Air-raid shelters and was now out of a job, except for voluntary fire duty in the streets. Eventually he went back to British Cyanides which had become British Industrial Plastics Ltd. My friend still worked at Typhoo who were asking for ex-staff to return. I applied and was taken on. Normally at this time it was not possible to change jobs at will, but Food had priority status. So I returned, not to the Packing Department but to the Blending and Bond.

Instead of the train I now travelled by Midland Red bus. The service, even in those difficult days was fairly reasonable, and the drivers and conductors, male and female, really did try to run the buses on time. It was known as the 'Friendly Midland Red' then. We got to know most of the staff, and they knew their regular passengers at all the bus stops, and they were not averse to tooting the horn to warn one who was not yet at the bus stop, either to break into a run, or to hop on to the bus. Cars and buses had their lamps masked too. Petrol was strictly rationed so there was not so much traffic about, but winter travelling was far from easy especially during the black-out. The bombing closed streets off many times and we made some strange detours, or we had delays as traffic was filtered through partly closed roads. Usually though I was home by a quarter to seven, delivered right to the door, cutting out altogether that long lonely walk across station Road and Britannia Road. Fog was one of the main hazards however. One night we walked all the way back. The fog was so thick that everything on wheels was brought to a halt in the City centre.

Within three months of going back to Typhoo there was a dreadful raid and the place was badly damaged internally, mostly by fire and water. We all congregated on the other side of the street as the brown smoke still curled up into the sky. I went back to help clean up the mess. Typical of the will of the people in those days, in a few short weeks the first of the automatic packers had been stripped down, cleaned and re-assembled, and was back in production.

The news elsewhere was not so good. Malta was being besieged and needing help badly. The Russian War with Finland ended but now they in turn were being invaded by the Germans. It was impossible to send help by land so our convoys had to go by the terrible Arctic route.

Arthur Southall married Edna Bird and they went to live in South Wales, near Cardiff.

There seemed to be war zones everywhere. Japan had joined Germany and Italy and finally in 1941 they attacked the U.S. Pacific Fleet at Pearl Harbour, and President Roosevelt, now in office for the third time, declared war on the Axis powers and promised a 'lease lend' system to Britain. When the American troops arrived in Great Britain we had visits at home from Aunt Phoebe's son Clarence, and her sons-in-law Bill Taylor and Carl Burns.

Despite all the fighting all around the world, it seems here at home things were quieter. Never having been able to go to Evening Classes I had taken some Correspondence courses but I now decided I would go to private classes and learn Shorthand/Typing. I was twenty four now and I needed to tackle something new. So for the next two years I went Tuesdays and Thursdays straight from work for two hours, seven to nine and through all the talk of the many battles, in Malta, the Western Desert between Rommel and Montgomery, I practiced my shorthand. When waves of planes went over now they were the R.A.F. bombers flying to attack Germany. Remembering the devastation of our own cities we still shuddered, but we knew it was something that had to be done.

By 1943 the tide seemed to be in favour of the Allies. The German army surrendered to Russia and America was doing well against Japan, with more than a little help from the Australians.

Unfortunately I had not been well for some time. I suffered repeated bouts of colitis and my diet was severely restricted which worried Mom as she was already troubled enough with the rationing. I gave up my lessons but only three weeks later I had a nervous breakdown. The doctor was not surprised, he said I had had neurasthenia for the last eighteen months. I had just over a week at home then he said he wanted me to get a job nearer home doing something totally different. He was a great believer in work therapy I think. I went to the Labour Exchange and they were not sure what to send me to do. Eventually, after we had chatted for a while the girl found I could do shorthand/typing even though I had never worked in an office, so with the doctors permission I applied for the post of General Clerk at a local Steel Merchants. Ironically, the first thing I had to do was book-keeping but I took to it like a duck taking to water. The two Mr. Shaws were kindness itself to me. Like a couple of Dutch uncles I became the 'little girl in our office'. They each had daughters of their own around my own age and they treated me the same. Each of them assured me that they had had nervous trouble themselves and quite understood how I felt.

Hilda left school at Christmas and went to work at the Co-op in Hawes Lane. She had always loved shops and used to help Mrs. Barnsley sometimes. In June came the D Day Landings. Rumours had been flying round thick and fast about all the troops and equipment along the south coast and at last it came true. The Second Front was opened and we learned of the oil pipe-line PLUTO laid along the bed of the channel and "the Mulberry Harbour to aid the Allied landings. Not everything was going our way however. The disastrous air-borne landing at Arnhem and the Vl and V2 bombs which began to fall without any warning were very upsetting.

However, this time there was no doubt that the Allies were winning the war. It was unfortunate that President Roosevelt who had been elected for a fourth term of office in 1944 died on the twelfth April 1945. It was obvious at the Yalta Conference that he was mortally ill.

Events happened fast in the final stages. The German Army surrendered in Italy. Three days later Russia captured Berlin. Hitler chose to commit suicide and on the eighth of May Germany surrendered unconditionally. This is now known as VE Day. A few days later the world reeled in horror as the concentration camps revealed their deadly secrets.

The war in the Eastern zone dragged on longer. Eventually it was decided by the powers that be that the atomic bomb be used. Millions of leaflets were dropped warning the people, then the first terrible bomb was dropped on Hiroshima on the sixth August. On the ninth a second bomb was dropped on Nagasaki. Next day the Japanese Government agreed to unconditional surrender. This was VJ Day.

The loss of life by the Japanese was horrific, but it undoubtedly saved the lives of countless Allied soldiers. If the Japanese had had such a bomb they would have had no compunction in using it, as witnessed by the atrocities committed by them against Prisoners of War. Equally as bad as the German concentration camps.

Following the announcements of cease fire both in May and August, street parties and celebrations were hastily arranged. Bonfires were lit and effigies of Hitler were burned instead of Guy Fawkes. Carefully hoarded little luxuries were brought out and people let their hair down. Victory parades were held everywhere. Relief and joy affect people in different ways. Some got drunk, and some went to church to offer prayers of thankfulness for our deliverance from evil.

Even though the war was over, life was still difficult. We had learned to 'Make do and Mend' and 'Dig for Victory', slogans used during the war. Everything that could be recycled was saved Paper, metal, rags, bones, rubber, and left over food scraps to feed pigs. We had eaten some curious concoctions, some quite tasty, some not so good. All the well-known food firms had come out with their own recipes, I still have a Stork recipe book, but we knew it would be a long time before things were back to pre-war days.

A general Election was held later in the year. Labour gained control. Winston Churchill ceased to be Prime Minister, Clement Attlee was now in charge.

For the last two years we had been going to Blackpool for our holidays. Instead of Aunt Martha and Emmie Baker taking me, I was pleased now to arrange this for them. It cost fourteen shillings a day (seventy pence in new money) for full board in 1946.

The doctor suggested that I go and learn to dance. I was still not as healthy as he would like me to be. I had settled down well at my new job. I could see now that I ought to have trained for office work before. Accountancy appealed to me tremendously, but I never believed in crying over spilt milk. I can't say I am altogether sorry about the other years. I love to know how to do things, and how goods are manufactured, and I think that anything learned is never totally wasted. I met some nice people, and made some good friends. Gladys Amos, nee Mason and I have just celebrated fifty years of friendship, to name but one.

Eventually I decided I would ask Hilda to go with me to learn to dance. Hilda could dance already, she used to go Saturday afternoons with her friends, but we never told Dad. However, when the doctor said he wanted me to go to meet more people, it wasn't that I didn't go out, but as he pointed out, going to the theatre or to the cinema didn't get me talking to other people and he said he wanted me to talk to strangers, no matter where I was, so Dad raised no objection.

So we joined a Dance Club, now the Adelphi at Blackheath. I found it very hard going at first. My nerves were in such a dreadful state, but gradually, helped by the patience and kindness of the Principals, Dorothy Darby, and Harry Hipkiss, and fellow pupils, I eventually won through. I shall always be very grateful. We were a close-knit little community at that time. We went out as a club, sometimes as many as forty or so of us.

Of course by now the forces began to be de-mobbed. Jack Southall had been in the R.A.F.. During the war he had married Jean Bache from Blackheath. He was the closest relative because they had been nearest to me all my life. They took the place of the brothers which I didn't have. I daresay I had other cousins in the forces, but I didn't know them.

Things were different now. Hundreds of troops, both sexes, had learned to drive during the war. They had driven in deserts, on autobahns, in convoys, and alone, and when they came home again they still wanted to drive. Their own cars this time.

This was a new generation. They were not tied now to either bus or train services. They were liberated from the time tables and waiting queues. Week-ends saw them setting off visiting resorts weekly, that pre-war had only been visited once or twice a year. Many a granny and grandad saw the sea then for the first time, and lots of other places of which they had previously only heard.

When we went to Dances now we had a taxi home instead of walking. Also at the Dance Club we met two rather special young men who had recently been de-mobbed. Both from Blackheath, I got married in 1949, Hilda in 1950, Both weddings at Rowley Church.

The Hadley Family Tree had thickened and thrust forth two new branches. As Dad said, he had gained the two sons he would have liked to have had. Leslie Harold Davies and Wallace Raymond Knight.

And now, for each of you, a new beginning.

Lightning Source UK Ltd.
Milton Keynes UK
UKOW030936050312

188364UK00001B/2/P